log cabin quilts with attitude

by sharon v. rotz

Published by

An Imprint of F+W Publications

700 East State Street • Iola, WI 54990-0001
715-445-2214 • 888-457-2873

Our toll-free number to place an order or obtain a free catalog is (800) 258-0929.

The following trademarked terms and companies appear in this publication:

Clover Needlecraft Inc., Hobbs Heirloom® Premium batting, Hobbs Thermore® batting, Steam-A-Seam®, Steam-A-Seam2®, The Warm™ Company, Wrights®, Prym™ Consumer USA, Omnigrid®, Collins®, Warm & White™, Lite Steam-A-Seam2®, June Tailor®, Sulky® of America, SOFTouch™ Quilt Hangers, EZ Quilting® by Wrights®, Michael Miller Fabrics, Robert Kaufman Fabrics.

Library of Congress Catalog Number: 2005934241

ISBN-13: 978-0-89689-308-5
ISBN-10: 0-89689-308-1

Designed by Elizabeth Krogwold
Edited by Susan Sliwicki

Printed in China

acknowledgments

Certainly this book would not have been possible without the help of the wonderful people who fill my life. My special thanks to:

- My family for their love and encouragement. Thanks to my husband, Tom, for balancing me and keeping me focused; to Steph and Jeff for always believing their mother can do anything; and to Katie and Chris for adding their support.
- The staff at Krause Publications, especially Candy Wiza, Julie Stephani and my editor, Susan Sliwicki, for their help in putting this book together.
- My quilting friends, Connie Biggar, Jan Sherman, Mary Sipiorski and Chris Kirsch, for sharing their inspiration, their quilts, their opinions and their technical advice — and for always being ready for a road trip.
- The Undercover Quilters and members of the Star Point Quilt Guild for keeping me quilting.

table of contents

introduction

My strips were a little wrinkled and slightly tangled inside a much-used cardboard box. Needless to say, she had great fun teasing me about my organizational skills.

Willing to rise to the occasion, I went home determined to straighten up my quilting life. After sorting through my stash, I realized how many unused strips of fabric I had left over from various projects. I enjoyed the memories that these strips brought to me, and I knew I wanted to combine them into a quilt.

As I pondered what is fun about making a quilt and what causes problems, I came up with guidelines for my quilt. I wanted to be free to:

- Combine all of my various fabrics in one quilt;
- Use all of my strips, as they were already cut;
- Disregard that perfect ¼" seam allowance;
- Avoid matching corners when putting blocks together;
- Eliminate ripping out mistakes;
- Quilt without hitting "lumps" from the seam allowance;
- Use my quilting templates without stretching or shrinking the quilting designs or figuring out corner designs; and
- Use up some of my stash, so I wouldn't feel guilty about buying fabulous new fabric.

I wanted a quilt project that was so easy, I could grab a bag of strips and sew any time I had 10 minutes to spare. The log cabin block was a familiar friend that used strips, so I started randomly picking up strips and sewing log cabin blocks.

Every quilt has its story, and the Freedom Quilt is no exception. So, grab a cup of coffee and relax as I share the story of the Freedom Quilt with you.

Once upon a time, I started down a new pathway into the land of quilting. Here I met a new quilting friend who had a special talent for organizing.

One day, we went on our first quilting adventure together. Her strips were neatly cut, layered and organized in a plastic storage box.

After making several blocks, I decided that they were colorful but rather boring. What my blocks needed was a bit of attitude. So, I thought of re-cutting them on an angle.

My blocks weren't the same size, because I was making these blocks from strips of varying widths. Therefore, I could cut using various angles — whatever angle I could fit on the block. My blocks suddenly developed a fun, carefree look with a whole lot of attitude. The freedom block was born.

My first freedom blocks were re-cut into squares, but that presented the dilemma of matching those corners when I put the blocks together. My first thought was to cut the blocks to different sizes, but how would I ever be able to sew the quilt together? A better solution would be to cut the blocks the same width but different lengths. I could easily sew the blocks together in long vertical rows, and then these rows could then be assembled into a quilt top.

When I stitched the rows together, they were uneven on the bottom because of the different lengths of the blocks. That was a problem for another day. Today was quilting day.

Keeping with my goal to avoid a lot of techni-

cal manipulating of design templates, I merely ran the design down the center of each vertical strip and off of the bottom. I even marked the design on the solid back of the quilt, which made the marking so much easier to see.

The second quilting problem I was trying to avoid was sewing over seam allowance "lumps." In a pieced quilt, it would be very difficult to avoid all the seams. By keeping my design 1" away from the vertical seam lines, I eliminated having to sew over the "lumpiest" areas of the quilt.

After finishing the quilting, it was on to the binding. What was I going to do with that uneven edge on the quilt bottom? With my husband's question "Why are quilts always square?" bouncing around in my head, I decided to leave it as it was. The uneven bottom added a fun touch and another bit of spunky attitude.

You, too, may be feeling the guilt of having one too many fabric strips and needing a little room for your new stash. If you are ready for a quilt with fewer rules and more fun, then the Freedom Quilt is for you! Don't be afraid to cut a few strips off of those new stash fabrics. It's surprising how a little will perk up the whole quilt!

about the author

Sharon V. Rotz is an experienced quilter, teacher, designer and textile artist.

Rotz has taught quilting for the past 20 years,

and she began teaching freedom quilting in 2000. Her prize-winning quilts have been featured in gallery art exhibits and regional and international shows. She also has sold her textile art to medical facilities, museums and numerous private collectors.

A graduate of the University of Wisconsin-Stout, Rotz has worked in the ready-made clothing industry, operated her own business creating custom soft furnishings and clothing and designed exclusive patterns for the Better Homes and Gardens Quilting Catalog. She began publishing her own pattern line, Bysher, in 1999.

A resident of Mosinee, Wis., Rotz enjoys inspiration and encouragement from her husband, Tom; her two married children and their spouses; and a growing number of grandchildren. When she's not quilting, Rotz enjoys spending time outdoors, especially fishing.

Visit her online at www.bysher.net.

chapter 1 learn the moves

You don't need a lot of equipment or lessons to get started making freedom blocks. Once you assemble some basic tools and learn a few techniques, you'll be ready to tackle the projects in this book.

Tools and Supplies

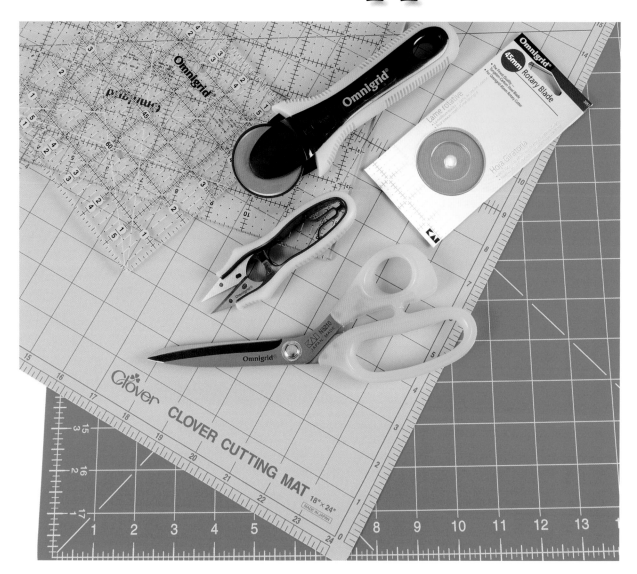

Here are the basic tools and supplies you'll need to get started with freedom quilting.

General Tools

The biggest tool necessity is a sewing machine complete with related accessories. Keep your machine in good working condition, and change needles often for the best results.

You'll also need an iron and ironing board. When you're working with appliqué, a pressing sheet will help to protect your iron.

Scissors, a rotary cutter, a ruler and a cutting mat are vital for quilting. A 12½"-square ruler will work to trim all of the blocks in this book, but you may find it more convenient to also have a 9½"- or 6½"-square ruler for some of the smaller blocks. Use masking tape to make easy-to-follow lines on your ruler.

Notions

Useful notions include thread in coordinating or contrasting colors, extra bobbins, spare needles, quilting pins, marking tools, a seam ripper and a bamboo stiletto.

Embellishments

Embellishments add extra flair to your projects. I used wire-edged ribbon to create the Flying Free Butterfly Pillow, and I embellished several projects with Wrights rickrack. I even used yarn to make piping.

The possibilities are endless for embellishments. Find inspiration in the brand-new yarns at your local knitting shop, raid your mom's stash for rickrack, or revel in the variety of choices at your local sewing store or quilt shop.

If you opt to machine quilt your own projects, you may wish to invest in tools and supplies to make that easier, such as specialty clips, quilting gloves or stencils. If you like piecing better than quilting, you may prefer to invest in building a good relationship with a talented machine quilter who can handle this step for you.

Fusible Web and Batting

You'll need paper-backed fusible web for the appliqué projects; I prefer Lite Steam-A-Seam2. Follow the manufacturer's suggestions for temperature settings, because some products have lower melting points than others.

I like cotton and cotton-blend battings, because they have rougher textures and don't shift in quilts, which makes it easier to machine quilt the finished piece. I find Hobbs Heirloom Premium Cotton Blend, an 80 percent cotton/20 percent polyester blend, is a good choice for both hand and machine quilting. A thinner batting, such as Thermore, is ideal for place mats or quilted tablecloths.

log cabin quilts with attitude

Fabrics

It's a given that you'll need fabric to complete your freedom blocks. You can splurge on the latest fabrics or raid your existing stash. Either way, the basics are the same: You'll need a square or rectangular center and plenty of strips to wrap around it.

I made only two rules for selecting fabrics for freedom blocks:

- I wouldn't use the same fabric twice in a row in the same block; and
- If I just couldn't stand the fabric combination, I would start a new block with that fabric strip.

Think About Centers

Square Centers

The right center for your block can be as simple as a square; any size will work. Of course, large center squares will get your blocks to grow bigger even faster. Faster is good, but sometimes, the center square needs to be small to be in proportion to the size of the finished block.

Rectangular Centers

Rectangles also can be used for centers to give a slight deviation to the plan.

Pieced Centers

Pieced centers add exciting interest to your log cabin blocks. Small paper-pieced blocks, four-patch blocks, nine-patch blocks, half-square triangles and flying geese blocks can be used. Again, be alert to the proportion of the center square to the final size of the log cabin block.

Pick Out Strips

When I began making freedom blocks, I found it easiest to pick out a center first, then randomly choose colors and fabric prints from my box of leftover strips.

The more blocks I made, the freer my color selections became. The blocks became more stimulating and exciting. And when I skewed the blocks and trimmed them on an angle, they shouted with newfound personality. Each and every project that I have made has become my new favorite.

Guard Your Strips Carefully

When I teach freedom blocks, I love to show students the fun of matching color randomly by pulling fabric strips out of a paper bag. After one class at a convention center, I carefully packed my strips and about 20 completed blocks in their paper bag and started carrying out my sewing equipment. Returning for my bag, I found that the janitors had come in and "cleaned" my fabric-filled bag, which was never to be seen again.

Basic Techniques

For the projects in this book, complete piecing with the right sides of the fabric together. Use a ¼" seam, unless otherwise indicated in the pattern. Press seam allowances together to one side, unless directed to press them open.

Make a Freedom Block

As long as there are individuals, there will be different approaches for making the familiar log cabin block, on which the freedom block is based. Here's the technique that I use to make freedom blocks.

1. Place the first strip right side up under the machine. Place a center piece wrong side up on the strip, and stitch a seam. The seam doesn't have to be an exact ¼", but you do want the seam to be straight. Too narrow of a seam allowance may pull apart, while too wide of a seam allowance will hide a lot of your beautiful fabric in the seam.

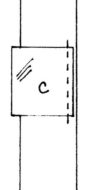

2. Press the seam allowance away from the center. Trim away the excess strip so it is even with the edge of the center.

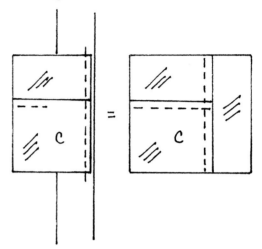

3. Place the second strip under the machine, right side up. Place the block right sides together on the strip with the first strip that you attached at the top. Stitch. Press away from the center and trim even with the edge of the block.

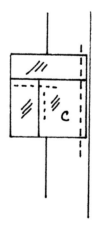

4. Place the third strip under the machine, right side up. Place the block on the strip right sides together with the second strip at the top. I always know that the last strip that I added to a block is always at the top; this strip has no seams crossing it. Stitch, trim even and press.

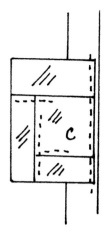

5. Place the fourth random strip under the machine, right side up. Place the block right sides together on the strip with the third strip at the top so the center is circled completely. Stitch, press and trim.

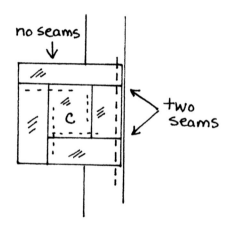

no seams

two seams

6. After making the first complete circle of the log cabin block, check your work. Place the block on strip No. 5. Look at the wrong side of the block; there will be no seam on the top edge and two seams on the stitching edge.

Tip

Make a mistake? Trim off the offending part of the block and start again; there is no need to rip your seams.

Tip

Lose your place when adding strips to a block? It's easy to figure out where to stitch next. Look at the wrong side of the block; there will be no seam on the top edge and two seams on the stitching edge. Now you can pick up any block at any time and know on which edge you should seam the next strip.

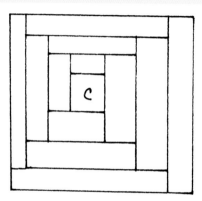

7. Continue to add random strips around the block; the block will begin to show its personality. The center of the block may no longer be in the middle because the strips on one side may be wider than the other.

8. Use a rotary cutter and ruler to shape up wavy edges on the block. If you feel that a strip is too wide after you have stitched it on, trim that strip down to size.

9. Add strips until the block is approximately 2" larger than the finished size required for the project.

Trim Freedom Blocks

Once you've finished adding strips to the block, it's time to trim it. Trimming transforms colorful, yet ordinary, log cabin blocks into freedom blocks with a lot of spunky attitude.

1. Determine the size of the blocks needed. For example: For 7½" x 7½" finished blocks in the quilt, cut each block to 8" x 8".

2. Choose a square ruler to trim around the block. If you don't have a square ruler that is the exact size of the desired block, choose a square ruler that is larger than the block size. Use tape to mark the correct cutting lines on the square.

3. Lay the marked ruler on the freedom block and decide whether you will want a left freedom block or a right freedom block.

Left Freedom Blocks

1. Lay the ruler on the block so that the ruler is tilted higher on the left side than it is on the right. Tilt the ruler to a random angle that fits the size of the block. If you can't tilt the block at least ½", add a few more strips to it. Too small of a cut angle will make the block look like a crooked square, while too large of an angle will put the block on point.

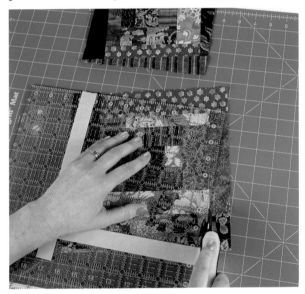

2. Make sure that you are cutting on the correct lines, that you have fabric under all of the corners of the taped lines, and that you have laid the square ruler at an interesting angle. Cut the two outer sides of the block.

Tip

Make it easy to tell right-skewed freedom blocks from left-skewed freedom blocks. Put a piece of colored tape on all of the right-skewed blocks, and you'll be able to pick them out easily when you begin assembling the quilt top.

3. Rotate the block 180 degrees, and line it up with the taped lines. Cut the other two sides of the block.

Right Freedom Blocks

1. Lay the ruler on your block so that it is tilted higher on the right side than it is on the left. Tilt the ruler to a random angle that fits the size of the block as you did for the left freedom block. If you can't tilt the block at least ½", add a few more strips to it. Too small of a cut angle will make the block look like a crooked square, while too large of an angle will put the block on point.

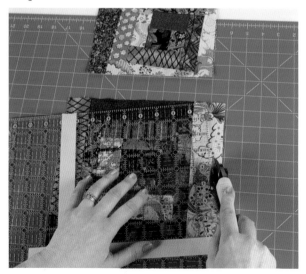

2. Make sure that you are cutting on the correct lines, that you have fabric under all of the

corners of the taped lines and that you have laid the square ruler at an interesting angle. Cut the two outer sides of the block.

3. Rotate the block 180 degrees, and line it up with the taped lines. Cut the other two sides of the block.

Rectangular Freedom Blocks

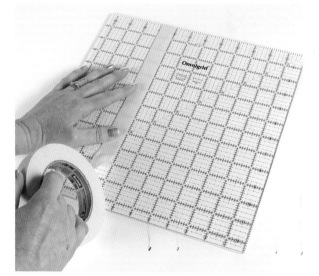

1. Tape the square ruler only for the width of the blocks. Each block will be cut at a different length.

2. Tilt the square ruler, and check the shortest length that is showing under the corner of the ruler. This is the maximum size for your block. If this is too small, go back to the sewing machine and add more strips to your block. Trim two sides of the block.

3. Rotate the block 180 degrees. Trim the other two sides of the block.

Cut and Piece Strips

Follow these guidelines to create the bias and binding strips you'll need for the projects in this book.

Bias Strips

Use bias strips for appliqué, because they are flexible and will curve easily to give a realistic look to your vines.

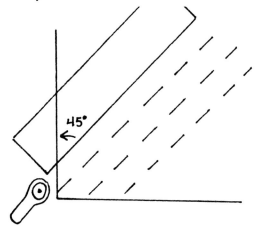

1. To cut bias strips, lay the fabric out on the cutting mat without folding it. Align the 45-degree line of the ruler with the straight edge of the fabric. Make a diagonal cut. Measure from this cut edge to cut bias strips the width needed for your project.

2. To piece the strips, align the strips right sides together on the ¼" stitching line. Stitch on the seam line, and press the seam allowance open.

Binding Strips

Use binding strips to add a nice, crisp edge to a quilt. Follow these guidelines for the straight-edge quilts featured in this book.

1. Cut the binding strips 2" wide and on the straight grainline. Cut enough strips to exceed the perimeter of the quilt.

2. While seated at your sewing machine, overlap the ends of two strips, both right side up, and cut them at an angle. This does not have

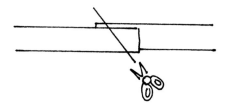

to be a precise 45-degree angle, but because you are cutting through both strips at the same time, it will be the same angle on both strips.

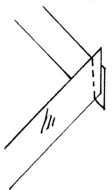

3. Align the strips at the ¼" seam allowance, and stitch a diagonal seam. Using a diagonal seam will spread the bulk of the seam allowance in the binding strip rather than having it concentrated at one "lumpy" spot.

4. Piece as needed. The length of your binding should be approximately 6" longer than your quilt circumference. Press the seam allowances open.

Add the Binding

A narrow binding gives a nice, crisp edge to the quilt. Wait to add the binding until you've finished quilting your piece and added a rod pocket, if desired.

1. Press the binding in half lengthwise, wrong sides together, to make a 1"-wide strip.

2. Match the raw edge of the binding to one raw edge of the quilt top, right sides together. Stitch a ¼" seam to attach the binding to the quilt.

3. Trim the batting and backing even with the seam allowance. Turn the folded edge of the binding over the raw edge of the quilt and around to the back of the quilt. Finish binding the quilt by hand, stitching it neatly to the back of the quilt.

Bind and Miter Outside Corners

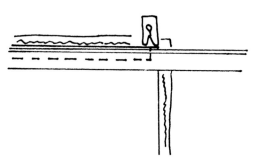

1. Leaving a 3" tail of binding, start stitching the binding along one side of the quilt. Match the raw edges of the binding to the edge of the quilt top, and stitch a ¼" seam. Stop stitching ¼" before the corner of the quilt. With the needle down, pivot the quilt to align with the second side of the quilt. Backstitch to the edge of the quilt top, roughly four to five stitches.

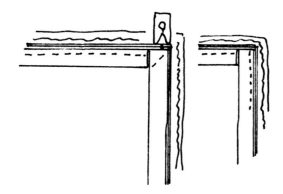

2. With the needle down, raise the presser foot, and fold the binding back to the needle and even with the second edge of the quilt; a stiletto or seam ripper may be helpful for this task. A 45-degree miter will form under the fold. Continue stitching the second side of the quilt.

3. Continue around the quilt. Trim the backing and batting even with the quilt top. Fold the binding around the edge to the quilt back to reveal the mitered corners. When hand stitching the binding to the quilt back, form a folded miter at the corners.

Bind and Miter Inside Corners

To have those interesting, uneven edges on your quilt, you will alternate inside corners with outside corners. After all, you can't have an inside corner without that outside corner. If you have never tried these before, you will find they are quite easy.

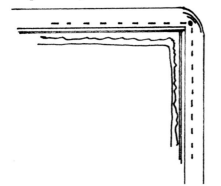

I. Stop stitching ¼" from the inside corner. With the needle down, pivot the quilt and align with the second side. Do not do any backstitching or allow any extra fabric for turning. Simply continue stitching along the second side. Because the fabric will not lay flat at the pivot, keep the edges even and avoid catching any excess binding in the stitching.

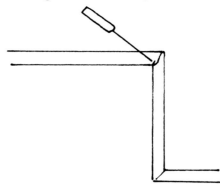

2. Clip the seam allowance at the corner pivot point and fold the binding to the quilt back. The binding should naturally fold into a mitered corner; if it doesn't, help it a little with your stiletto or seam ripper.

Join the Ends of the Binding

This method is much quicker and easier than most methods, yet it yields neat results.

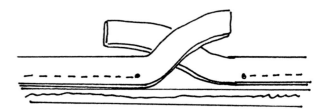

I. Start stitching the binding on, leaving a 3" unstitched tail of binding. Stitch the binding on around your quilt and stop 3" to 4" from your starting point. Remove the quilt from the machine.

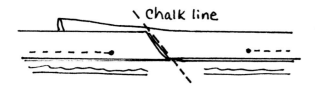
Chalk line

2. Trim the starting end on a diagonal. You will not have to open the fold. Lay this end over the finish end and draw a pencil or chalk line at the overlap.

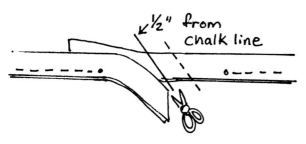
½" from chalk line

3. Trim the binding ½" longer than this drawn line.

4. Align the folded binding ends at the ¼" seam line and stitch. Backstitch at the folded edge. Open the seam allowance.

5. The binding should now fit exactly to the quilt edge. Stitch the binding in place, overlapping previous seams to secure the stitching.

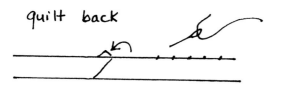
quilt back

6. Turn to the back and hand stitch, trimming or tucking under the seam allowance tail.

Use Two Fabrics with Overlapping Corners

Here's another technique you may wish to try for binding your quilts.

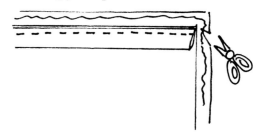

1. Match the raw edges of the underlap binding (fabric 1) to the edge of the quilt top, and start stitching the binding on at the corner edge of the quilt. Stitch a ¼" seam to the opposite corner of the quilt and off the edge. Trim the batting and backing even with the quilt top. Trim the ends of the underlap binding even with the sides of the quilt top. Turn the binding to the back, and hand stitch it before attaching the overlap binding.

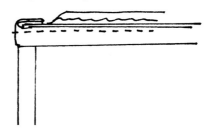

2. Match the raw edges of the overlap binding (fabric 2) to the edge of the quilt top, extending the binding ½" to ¾" beyond the edge of the quilt top. Fold the end of the overlap binding snugly around the edge to the back of the quilt. This will encase the previously bound edge of the quilt. Use a ¼" seam to stitch the binding to the quilt edge. Before you get to the opposite end, trim the binding ½" to ¾" longer than the quilt top, and fold the binding around to the quilt back. Finish stitching the binding to the quilt edge, catching in the binding that was folded to the back.

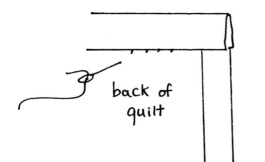

3. Trim the batting and backing even with the quilt top. Turn the binding to the quilt back, and hand stitch the binding and folded ends.

Add a Rod Pocket

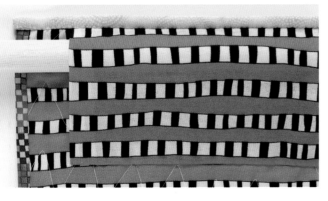

Add the rod pocket to your quilt after you have stitched the binding to the front of the quilt and trimmed the excess batting and backing.

1. Cut a strip of fabric 8½" wide by 2" less than the width of the quilt. Finish the ends of the rod pocket by folding the ends over ½" to the wrong side of the fabric and fusing them in place with a narrow piece of fusible web. Press the fabric strip in half lengthwise, wrong sides together.

2. Center the rod pocket strip on the back of the quilt with the raw edges even with the top of the quilt. Stitch a ¼" seam to secure the rod pocket to the back of the quilt; you will be stitching over the seam that you used to apply the binding to the front of the quilt.

3. Fold the binding to the back of the quilt and hand stitch. Hand stitch the bottom of the rod pocket to the back of the quilt. Be careful that your stitches do not come through to the right side of the quilt.

Add a Label

A label adds the perfect finishing touch to any project you make. It's a great place to sign your quilt. It also can share the quilt's name, the year it was made, your name and address, or even something as simple as care instructions, if the quilt is a gift.

There are a variety of products on the market that make it easy to label your quilt. Or, you can easily make your own with fabric-safe markers, a scrap of fabric and some fusible web.

chapter 2 freedom quilting

Do you have boxes of leftover strips that you just couldn't throw away? Do these fabrics bring to mind special moments? Do you still love the colors and designs? Then it's time to combine these fabrics into colorful, never-fail freedom blocks.

Freedom Quilt

Materials

Fabric

8 yd. assorted medium to dark fabrics (freedom blocks and heading)

¾ yd. navy (border and binding)

⅛ yd. red (piping)

5½ yd. solid red (backing)

Other Supplies

68" x 94" batting

2 yd. acrylic yarn (piping)

12" square ruler for trimming bocks

Walking foot for your sewing machine (optional)

General sewing tools and supplies

Finished size: 63" x 90". Shown with Freedom Pillows featured on page 24.

This is a great project to work on when you have only a few minutes to sew, because the blocks are easy and you have no specific measurements or complicated piecing to remember.

The object of this quilt is to use your excess stash. You can use small, paper-pieced blocks you've made, or bits and pieces of blocks that were left from other projects. Small blocks can be used for the centers of freedom blocks, and large extra blocks can be cut into strips to add interest around a solid center.

You can make your project any size; therefore, it is hard to determine the exact yardage you will use in your Freedom Quilt. You can always add new fabrics to the mix as you go. Get started and see where your path leads.

Cut

FABRIC	CUT	FOR
Assorted Medium to Dark	35 squares, 3½" x 3½"	Heading
	112 squares, 2" x 2"	Heading
	Strips, as needed, 1¼" to 3½" wide	Freedom blocks
Navy	2 strips, 2" x fabric width	Border
	8 strips, 2" x fabric width; piece the strips to a length of 312"	Binding
Red	2 strips, 1" x width of fabric	Piping

Construct

Make 70 blocks

1. Gather your strips into a brown paper bag, plastic storage container or cardboard box.

2. Select the centers for your blocks. These can be squares, rectangles, tiny four-patch blocks, stars or paper-pieced miniature blocks. The minimum center size is about 2" x 2" for this project, or you will never get a block made. The maximum center size is approximately 4" x 4"; otherwise, you'll have little room for additional strips.

3. Randomly pick a strip. With right sides together, stitch a center to one side of the strip. Press and trim the strip even with the center. Continue to add strips around the freedom block. Refer to Basic Techniques for detailed instructions. You may notice that the center of the freedom block is no longer in the middle of the block. This happens when you add wider strips on one side and narrower strips on another side. This is OK; your quilt is just starting to show its attitude.

4. Press the block. If a block doesn't look straight after pressing, use a rotary cutter to trim it up a bit. There is no need to unpick seams in this project; just trim off the offending part.

5. Consider how large you want the blocks to be. You will want the untrimmed blocks to be approximately 2" larger than the desired trimmed size. The length of each block is different, so when the rows are joined, you don't have to worry about matching the blocks to adjacent rows. In the Freedom Quilt shown, all of the blocks were trimmed to 9½" wide so they could be assembled in vertical rows; the lengths of the blocks ranged from 5½" to 11½", with most of the blocks measuring 7" to 9" long.

6. Trim the blocks; skew half to the left and the other half to the right. Refer to Trim Freedom Blocks for detailed instructions. Put a piece of colored tape on all of the right-skewed blocks so it will be easy to pick them out later.

Tip

Work on several freedom blocks at one time, so you won't have to keep popping up to press after each seam. I like to work on four blocks and continue to start new blocks until I have about 12 all at different stages of construction. This way, I can use the same fabric in several blocks but have it placed differently in each block. When I do get up for my pressing "stretch break," I have several blocks to press.

Assemble

Quilt Top

1. **Vertical Rows 1, 3, 5, 7:** Start at the top of the row with a right freedom block, and move down the row alternating right, left, right, left, etc., until you have a length of approximately 80" (nine or 10 freedom blocks).

2. **Vertical Rows 2, 4, 6:** Start at the top of the row with a left freedom block, and move down the row alternating left, right, left, right, etc., until you have a length of approximately 80" (nine or 10 freedom blocks).

3. Lay out the quilt before stitching the rows to adjust the color distribution and space the zingers to pop out around the quilt. As you move blocks around, be sure to trade left blocks with left blocks and right blocks with right blocks.

4. Let the quilt show its attitude with that carefree uneven bottom. Each row should have a difference in length of ¾" to 2". You may need to adjust some rows; trade blocks with other rows, or do some trimming. You can trim the blocks or trim at the top or the bottom of a row after stitching the blocks into rows. The rows in the quilt shown were 78¾", 78", 80", 79¼", 80", 77¼" and 78". If an uneven bottom edge doesn't appeal to you, cut all of the rows the same length. After all, it's your Freedom Quilt.

Rows

1	2	3	4	5	6	7
R	L	R	L	R	L	R
L	R	L	R	L	R	L
R	L	R	L	R	L	R
L	R	L	R	L	R	L
R	L	R	L	R	L	R
L	R	L	R	L	R	L
R	L	R	L	R	L	R
L	R	L	R	L	R	L
R	L	R	L	R	L	R
		L	R	L	R	R

5. Join the blocks, and then join the vertical rows. Avoid stretching the blocks by laying the rows on a flat surface and pinning them together before stitching. Use an even-feed or walking foot to stitch the rows together.

6. Staystitch a row of slightly longer stitches (length -3.0) around the quilt top to prevent the blocks or rows from pulling apart as you handle the quilt top. Keep the stitching less than ¼" from the edge, so it will be hidden in the binding.

Quilt Heading

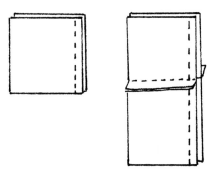

1. Use the 2" squares to piece 28 four-patches. With right sides together, seam two squares. Match this unit, right sides together, to another unit of two squares. Press seam allowances in opposite directions so they fit tightly together. Stitch and press the four-patch.

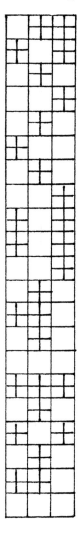

2. Lay out the 3½" squares and four-patches as shown, and stitch them to make the heading for the Freedom Quilt. In the quilt pictured, I replaced two squares with two stars that were left from another project.

3. Piece the 2" navy border strips, trim to 63½" and add them to the bottom of the pieced heading. Press the seam allowance to the navy border.

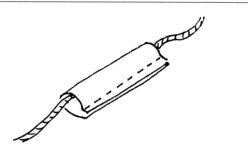

4. Piece the 1" red piping strips and trim to 63½". Press the strips in half lengthwise with wrong sides together. Insert a piece of yarn in the fold. Baste the piping to the bottom of the navy border, keeping raw edges even.

5. Pin the heading to the quilt top, right sides together. Stitch. Press the seam allowance toward the navy border. On the right side, the red piping strip will be toward the pieced freedom blocks.

Finish

1. Piece the backing and trim to 67" x 99".

2. Layer the quilt top, batting and backing. Baste. Quilt in the ditch between the navy border and the red piping on the top border. Quilt in the ditch between the navy border and the pieced header.

3. Because the quilt top is wonderfully busy with color and pattern, ornate quilting will not show. Save it for another project. Repeating designs, such as cable or crosshatching, will complement the top nicely. To prevent the chance of breaking needles, avoid quilting over the areas of greatest thickness, namely where the rows are joined together. Draw chalk lines 1" from the sides of rows 2, 4, and 6. Quilt these lines, starting from the red piping to the quilt bottom.

4. Cross hatch (diagonal lines) 1½" apart between the vertical lines. The crosshatching may be easier to mark and quilt from the back of the quilt. Quilt from the piping and run right off the bottom edge of the quilt.

5. On rows 1, 3, 5, and 7, quilt a 7"-wide cable. Again, this may be easier to mark and stitch from the back of the quilt. Quilt from the red piping right off the bottom of the quilt.

6. Mark a cable or other desired design across the heading. Center the design and work to the edges. Quilt.

7. Piece the remaining navy strips to use for the binding. Refer to Basic Techniques for detailed instructions.

Variation
Freedom Quilts With Sashing

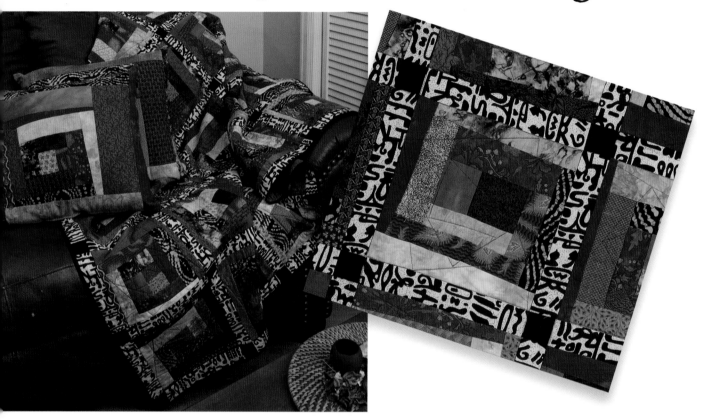

"Out of Africa" throw-size quilt and coordinating pillows by Mary Sipiorski.

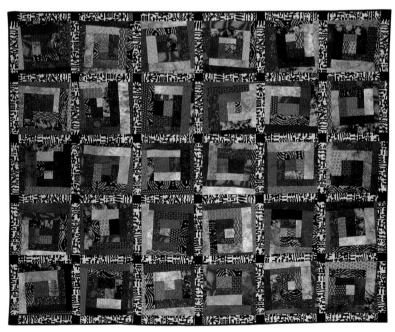

Those of you who are more organized may feel that the original Freedom Quilt is a bit too free. The perfect answer may be a Freedom Quilt With Sashing.

Two of my quilting friends, Mary Sipiorski and Jan Sherman, chose to separate the blocks in their quilts with sashing and cornerstones. This wonderful solution results in colorful, energetic freedom quilts with a bit of restraint.

The basic plan is to trim the blocks to 9½" x 9½", skewing blocks left and right. Cut 2" x 9½" sashing rectangles and 2" x 2" cornerstones.

"Traditional Treasures" queen-size quilt by Jan Sherman.

Freedom Pillows

Materials

Fabric (2 pillows)

1 yd. assorted medium- to dark-colored fabrics, or scrap strips left from previous projects (freedom blocks)

1¼ yd. muslin (pillow linings)

⅝ yd. red (pillow backs)

½ yd. blue (piping)

Other Supplies

2 pillow forms, 18" x 18"

20" x 40" batting

4½ yd. cotton filler cord, ³⁄₁₆" (4.8 mm) in diameter (piping)

9½" square ruler for trimming blocks

Zipper foot

General sewing tools and supplies

Finished size: 18" x 18"; set of two.

Nothing brightens up a room faster than adding a new pillow or two. Enjoy remembering past projects as you combine fabrics for these Freedom Pillows. It's easy to decorate throughout the year by incorporating seasonal fabrics with those already coloring your world. Piping makes a great finishing touch for the pillows, but it can be eliminated for faster construction.

Cut

FABRIC	CUT	FOR
Assorted medium to dark	As needed, strips 1¼" to 3" wide	Freedom blocks
Muslin	4 squares, 20" x 20"	Pillow linings
Red	2 squares, 20" x 20"	Pillow backs
Blue	2 bias strips, 1¾" wide; piece as needed to make strips 75" long	Piping
Batting	2 squares, 20" x 20"	Batting

Construct

Pillow Tops

1. Construct eight freedom blocks, each measuring 10" to 12" square before trimming. Trim each block to 9½" square; skew four blocks left and four blocks right. Refer to Basic Techniques for detailed instructions.

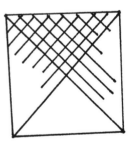

2. Stitch the blocks into four patches, alternating the left- and right-skewed blocks. Press. Make two.

3. On the muslin lining, draw pencil lines diagonally from corner to corner. Using these lines as a starting point, draw a series of parallel lines that are 1½" apart to form a diagonal grid, or cross hatching. Mark two.

4. Layer the muslin (drawn lines facing down), batting and pillow top (facing up). Pin through the center and corners, aligning the pieces on the muslin grid. Flip the unit muslin side up, and pin it for quilting. Remember to remove the aligning pins. Make two.

5. Quilt by stitching on the drawn lines. Since you are stitching from the muslin side, your bobbin thread will show on the pillow top, so plan the thread color accordingly. Trim the excess batting and muslin. Make two.

Piping

1. Stitch enough 1¾"-wide bias strips together to create a 75" length. Press the seams open.

2. Wrap the 75" strip around a 75" length of cotton cord; keep the right side of strip on the outside. Use a zipper foot to baste close to the cord.

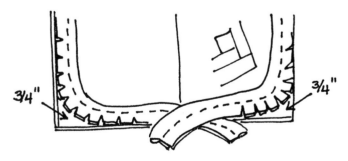

3. Starting in the center of one side of the pillow, pin piping to right side of a quilted pillow top. Match the raw edges of the piping with the raw edges of the pillow top. Clip the piping seam allowance at the corners. To give better shape to the pillow, round the corners as shown. Machine baste the piping onto the pillow top.

Assemble and Finish

I. Pin or baste the two remaining muslin squares to the wrong side of the pillow backs. This layer adds strength to the pillow backs to balance the quilted tops.

2. With right sides together, layer the pillow tops over the backs. Stitch around the pillow, ½" from the edge (close to the piping). Leave a 12" opening for turning. Trim.

3. Turn the pillow right side out, and insert a pillow form. Neatly stitch the opening closed.

Stand Tall America Banner

Materials

Fabric

2 yd. assorted medium to dark red and blue fabrics (freedom blocks)

1 yd. gold (star blocks, piping and binding)

¾ yd. assorted dark blues (star background and top border)

⅛ yd. red print (border)

2⅛ yd. backing

Other Supplies

4 yd. white or gold acrylic yarn (piping)

27" x 72" cotton batting

Tracing paper

Pencil

12" square ruler for trimming blocks

General sewing tools and supplies

4" Star and 5" Star Paper-Piecing Foundations on pages 118 & 119

Finished size: 23" x 69".

Announce your patriotic spirit in waves of red, blue and gold. Celebrate your freedom as you proudly display this quilt on your front door or in your entry. The Stand Tall America Banner combines freedom blocks with a top border of paper-pieced stars. Learn how to make your edges "wave" with pseudo-piping, and check out a paper-piecing technique to ensure that you have enough fabric to cover that paper.

Cut

FABRIC	CUT	FOR
Medium to dark red and blue	As needed, strips 1¼" to 2½" wide	Freedom blocks
Gold	2" bias strips; piece as needed to get 210" length	Binding
	2 bias strips 1" x 72"; piece as needed to get 72" length	Piping
Dark blues	1 strip, 1½" by 26"	Top border
	3 rectangles, 2½" x 4½"	Star spacers
	2 rectangles, 1½" x 5½"	Star spacers
	2 rectangles, 2¼" x 6½"	Vertical spacers
Red	1 strip, 2" x 26"	Border

Construct

Paper-Pieced Stars

Make three 4" stars and two 5" stars

1. Use tracing paper to trace three of each section of the 4" Star Paper-Piecing Foundations and two of each section of the 5" Star Paper-Piecing Foundations on pages 118 and 119.

2. Use an empty needle (no thread) to stitch on all of the lines of the paper-piecing foundations to perforate the paper. This will help you to remove the paper foundations later.

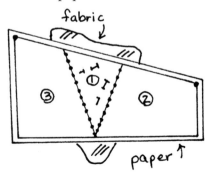

3. Center fabric 1 wrong side up under the paper so it completely covers position 1 and at is least ¼" larger than the pattern on all sides. Pin securely.

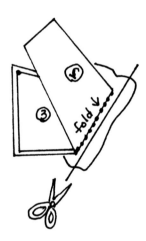

4. Fold the paper back on the perforated line between 1 and 2. Trim seam allowance to ¼".

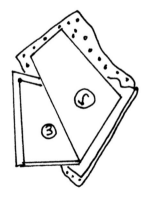

5. Align fabric 2 right sides together with fabric 1 and even with the seam allowance. Make sure that fabric 2 completely covers the area under the folded-back paper.

6. Unfold the paper. Stitch on the line between 1 and 2. Shorten your stitch length (1.5) to make paper removal easier.

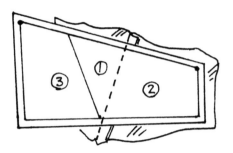

7. Press open the fabric covering the area under position 2.

8. Fold the paper back on the perforated line between 1 and 3. Trim the seam allowance to ¼". Align the third fabric right sides together, even with the seam allowance.

9. Make sure that fabric 3 completely covers the area under the folded-back paper. Unfold the paper, then stitch on the line between 1 and 3.

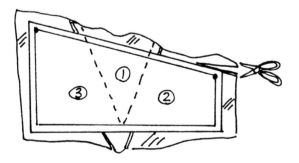

10. Press open the fabric covering position 3. Trim the block section on all sides.

11. Continue to make the three sections for each block.

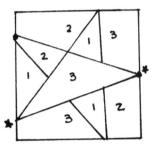

12. Stitch the sections together, matching the dots. To prevent stretching, leave the paper on the stars until you have completed the top border. Make five star blocks.

Freedom Blocks
Make 21 blocks

1. Refer to Basic Techniques for detailed information. For this project, you'll want the blocks to measure approximately 10" to 12" before trimming. Trim the blocks to 8½" wide by varying lengths of 8" to 10". Skew 11 blocks to the left and 10 to the right.

2. Arrange the blocks in three vertical rows of seven blocks each. Start Rows 1 and 3 with left blocks, and alternate with right blocks. Start Row 2 with a right block, and alternate with left blocks.

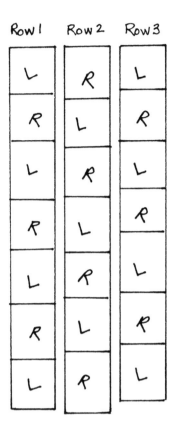

3. Stitch the vertical rows. Press.

Pseudo-Piping

This piped trim is soft, and it works very well on quilts. The yarn gives the piping a little body without the bulk.

1. Fold the 1"-wide bias strips in half lengthwise, wrong sides together, and press.

2. Insert yarn in the fold of each bias strip. Machine baste the edges together ⅛" from raw edges to form the piping.

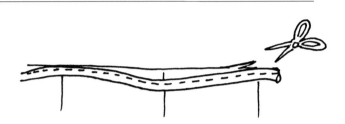

3. Pin the piping on the right edge of Row 1, which is the side between Rows 1 and 2. The raw edges of the piping will be toward the raw edge of the row. Curve the piping slightly as you pin to get the waves to form. Leave 3" of excess piping on the bottom of the row. Stitch the piping in place. Trim the seam allowance, but leave the excess piping.

4. Press the piping to the outside of the row, and press the seam allowances toward the block center.

5. Lay Row 1 next to and slightly on top of Row 2; check to ensure that you are overlapping enough to catch the bottom layer when you stitch.

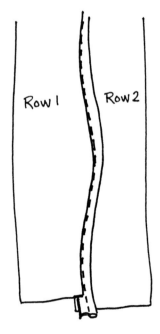

6. Stitch in the ditch to join Rows 1 and 2. Trim off the excess piping.

7. Repeat to attach Row 2 to Row 3.

Assemble

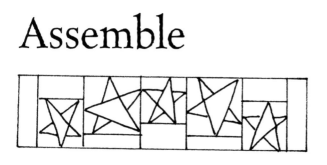

1. Add the star spacers as shown, and stitch the star border.

2. Add the 1½" x 26" blue strip to the top of the star border. Add the 2" x 26" red strip to the bottom of the star border. Press the seam allowances toward the solid strips. Remove the paper foundations from the stars.

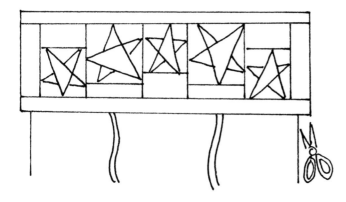

3. Center the top border on the quilt body. Stitch. Trim the border even with the edges of the quilt body.

Finish

1. Sandwich the backing, batting and quilt top. Baste the layers together.

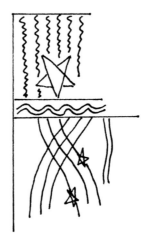

2. Quilt the banner. You may design your own quilting patterns, or you can try these ideas. In the body of the quilt, stitch a free-motion cable and randomly add stars. In the red border, stitch horizontal waving lines. Stitch in the ditch around the stars, and quilt wavy vertical lines in the background.

3. Bind the quilt with the 2"-wide bias strips. Curve the binding to make waves as you apply it to the body of the quilt. Refer to Basic Techniques for detailed instructions: Binding and Mitering Outside Corners and Binding and Mitering Inside Corners.

4. Add a rod pocket to the back of your quilt for easy hanging. Refer to Basic Techniques for detailed instructions.

Expand on the beauty of freedom blocks by incorporating pieced blocks into your designs. The charming Patio Party pieces will add a colorful and classy touch to your next outdoor party, while the Day Away projects are the perfect way to pamper yourself when you take a well-deserved break at your favorite park or festival.

Patio Party Wall Quilt

Materials

Fabric

2 yd. assorted medium- to dark-colored fabrics (freedom blocks)

1¼ yd. light blue (background, binding)

½ yd. multicolored print (lantern tops)

½ yd. assorted prints (lantern bottoms)

¼ yd. small check (binding)

⅛ yd. black (lantern ends)

1½ yd. backing, 42" wide

Other Supplies

2½ yd. red medium rickrack

2½ yd. yellow medium rickrack

44" x 48" batting

Invisible thread to attach rickrack

9" or larger square ruler

General sewing tools and supplies

Finished size: 40" x 44".

What's a better way to celebrate summer than to share time with your friends? Break out some snacks and tall, cool drinks, and throw a patio party. Add some colorful excitement with a Patio Party Wall Quilt. Make the quilt, hang it, and then relax with your friends as you enjoy some well-earned praise for your artwork.

Round out this playful look by making the coordinating table accessories featured on pages 50 through 61.

Cut

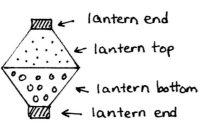

← lantern end
← lantern top
← lantern bottom
← lantern end

FABRIC	CUT	FOR
Assorted medium and dark	As needed, strips 1¼" to 2½" wide	Freedom blocks
Light blue	1 strip, 8½" x width of fabric, into: • 20 rectangles, 1¼" x 8½" • 5 rectangles, 2" x 8½"	Lantern blocks Border spacers
	2 strips, 3¾" x width of fabric	Lantern ends
	3 strips, 3¾" x width of fabric, into: • 40 rectangles, 3" x 3¾"	Lantern blocks
	2 strips, 2" x width of fabric, into: • 9 rectangles, 2" x 2½" • 1 rectangle, 2" x 4" • 1 rectangle, 2" x 2"	Borders Borders Borders
	2 strips, 2" x width of fabric	Top and bottom binding
Multicolored print	10 rectangles, 3" x 7"	Lantern tops
Assorted prints	10 rectangles, 3" x 7"	Lantern bottoms
Black	1 strip, 2" x width of fabric	Lantern ends

Construct

Lantern Blocks

Make 10 blocks

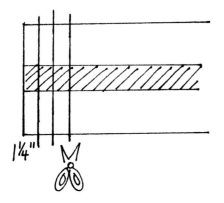

1¼"

1. To make the lantern ends, sew a 3¾" background strip to each side of the black 2" strip. Press the seams to the black strip. This unit should now measure 8½". Crosscut the unit into 20 rectangles, 1¼" x 8½".

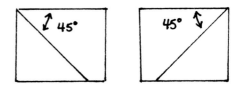

45° 45°

2. Draw diagonal stitching lines on the wrong side of the 3" x 3¾" background rectangles. Use the 45-degree line on your ruler, and draw from the corner of the block as shown. Mark 10 regular background rectangles and 10 reversed background rectangles.

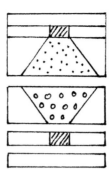

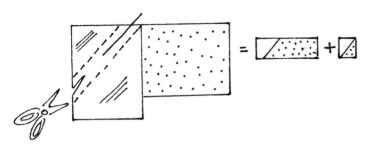

3. With right sides together, align a marked background on a lantern top as shown. Stitch on the drawn line. Check to see that the block is correct before stitching the second line. Stitch a second line ½" from the first. This second stitching line always should be toward the outside corner of the block. Cut between the two stitching lines. You have constructed a half-square triangle for your border in addition to the first corner of your lantern block. Press the seams toward the center of the block.

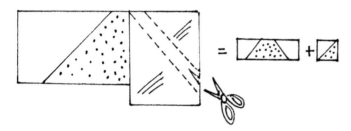

4. With right sides together, align a reversed marked background on the lantern top as shown. Stitch on the drawn line. Stitch a second line ½" toward the outside corner. Cut between the stitching lines. Press the seams toward the center of the block. Make 10 lantern tops.

5. Repeat the technique to make the lantern bottoms. Use the assorted lantern bottom fabrics and the remaining marked background rectangles and reversed marked background rectangles. Remember to make half-square triangles. Press the seams away from the center. Make 10 lantern bottoms.

6. Piece the block as shown. Start piecing from the center, and work to the top and bottom of the block. Press the seams away from the center. Make 10 blocks, 8½" x 8½".

Freedom Blocks
Make 15 blocks

1. Refer to Basic Techniques for general block construction instructions.

2. For this project, construct blocks that measure approximately 10" before trimming. Trim the blocks to 8½" x 8½". Skew eight blocks left and seven right.

Top and Bottom Borders

1. Gather all of the half-square triangles that you made when constructing the lantern blocks. Trim the half-square triangles to 2" x 2".

2. Piece the borders as listed, adding background squares and rectangles. Refer to the quilt layout diagram for additional information.

Row 1-Top: Two half-square triangles, 2½" rectangle, half-square triangle, 2" square.

Row 1-Bottom: Two half-square triangles, 2½" rectangle, two half-square triangles. Add a 2" x 8½" strip to bottom.

Row 2-Top: Half-square triangle, 2½" rectangle, three half-square triangles. Add a 2" x 8½" strip to top.

Row 2-Bottom: Two half-square triangles, 2½" rectangle, two half-square triangles.

Row 3-Top: Half-square triangle, 2½" rectangle, three half-square triangles.

Row 3-Bottom: Half-square triangle, 2½" rectangle, three half-square triangles. Add a 2" x 8½" strip to bottom.

Row 4-Top: Two half-square triangles, 2½" rectangle, two half-square triangles. Add a 2" x 8½" strip to top.

Row 4-Bottom: Half-square triangle, 2½" rectangle, three half-square triangles.

Row 5-Top: Half-square triangle, 4" rectangle, two half-square triangles.

Row 5-Bottom: Two half-square triangles, 2½" rectangle, two half-square triangles. Add a 2" x 8½" strip to bottom.

Assemble

1. Assemble the quilt in five vertical rows, starting with the top border, alternating three freedom blocks and two lantern blocks, and ending with the bottom border. You also will alternate freedom blocks as follows:

Rows 1, 3 and 5: Top border, freedom block-left, lantern, freedom block-right, lantern, freedom block-left, bottom border.

Rows 2 and 4: Top border, freedom block-right, lantern, freedom block-left, lantern, freedom block-right, bottom border.

2. Stitch the rows together.

3. To "hang" the lanterns, twist red and yellow rickrack together. Lay the twisted rickrack flat, and pin it to the top of the lanterns. A little sag between the lanterns will add to the hanging effect. Use invisible thread to stitch the rickrack in place.

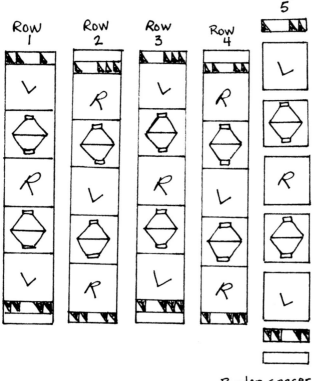

Border spacer

Finish

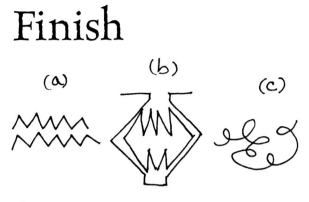

2. Bind the sides of the quilt with the checked strips, piecing as needed. Bind the top and bottom of the quilt with the background fabric. Refer to Basic Techniques for binding instructions: Using Two Fabrics with Overlapping Corners.

1. Sandwich the backing, batting and quilt top. Baste the layers together. You can create original quilting designs, or you an try these ideas. Quilt random zigzag lines across the freedom blocks (a), outline the lantern blocks (b), and have fun "looping" the background (c).

3. Add a rod pocket to the top of the wall hanging. Refer to Basic Techniques for detailed instructions.

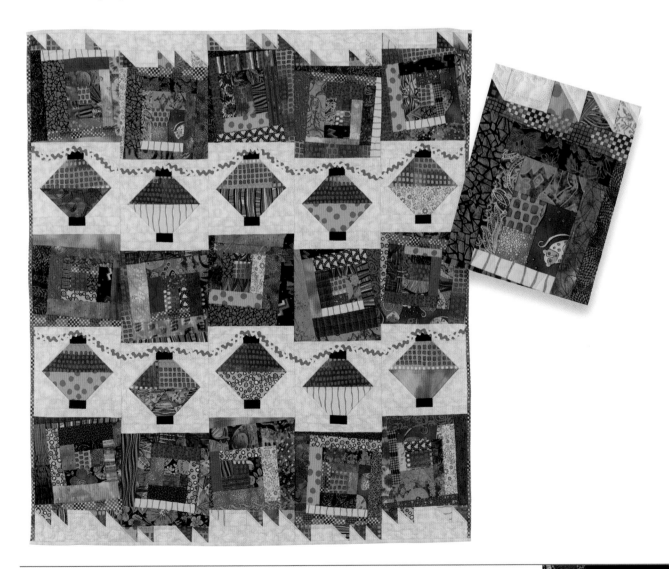

Patio Party Quilted Tablecloth

Materials

Fabric

2 yd. assorted medium- to dark-colored fabrics (freedom blocks)

2½ yd. light blue (center, block background, binding)

½ yd. multicolored print (lantern tops)

½ yd. assorted prints (lantern bottoms)

⅛ yd. black (lantern ends)

3½ yd. backing fabric

Other Supplies

60" x 60" low-loft batting

5 yd. red medium rickrack

5 yd. yellow medium rickrack

Invisible thread (attaching rickrack, quilting)

9" or larger square ruler

General sewing tools and supplies

Finished size: 56" x 56".

Bring good cheer and great food to the table with the Patio Party Quilted Tablecloth. Freedom blocks and lanterns add a festive touch to your table. The lanterns "hang" from colorful rickrack cords that are so authentic, they even include that one knot in the cord that never seems to come out.

Cut

FABRIC	CUT	FOR
Assorted medium and dark	As needed, strips 1¼" to 2½" wide	Freedom blocks
Light blue	1 square, 40½" x 40½"	Background
	1 strip, 8½" x width of fabric, into: • 24 rectangles, 1¼" x 8½"	Lantern blocks
	2 strips, 3¾" x width of fabric	Lantern ends
	4 strips, 3¾" x width of fabric, into: • 48 rectangles, 3" x 3¾"	Lantern blocks
	6 strips, 2" x width of fabric	Binding
Multicolored print	3 strips, 3" x width of fabric, into: • 12 rectangles, 3" x 7"	Lantern tops
Assorted prints	12 rectangles, 3" x 7"	Lantern bottoms
Black	1 strip, 2" x width of fabric	Lantern ends

Construct

Lantern Blocks

Make 12 blocks

I. Refer to Patio Party Wall Quilt for instructions to construct the lantern blocks. Make 12 lantern blocks, 8½" x 8½".

Freedom Blocks

Make 12 blocks

I. Refer to Basic Techniques for detailed instructions. For this project, construct blocks that measure approximately 10" before trimming. Trim each block to 8½" x 8½"; skew six blocks left and six right.

Assemble

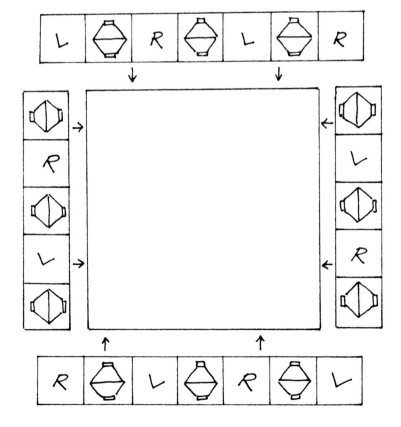

1. Lay out the tablecloth center. Place a left freedom block in the first corner, and alternate the freedom blocks and lantern blocks around the center. Alternate the skew of the freedom blocks, and place the bottoms of the lantern blocks along the outside of the quilt. Stitch opposite sides to the tablecloth center. Stitch the remaining sides.

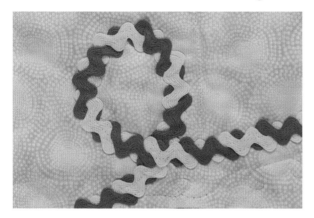

2. To "hang" the lanterns, twist red and yellow rickrack, lay it flat, and pin it to the top of the lanterns. For authenticity, add that little knot that never straightens out. To piece the rickrack, start the rickrack on the center block of one side and pin, ending at the center block on the opposite side. Open the seam a few stitches at the top of these two center blocks, tuck the ends of the rickrack in the seam and re-stitch the seam. Use invisible thread to stitch the rickrack in place.

Finish

1. Piece the backing, and cut it to 60" x 60".

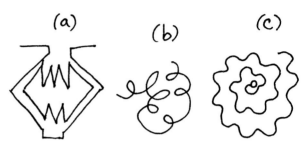

(a) (b) (c)

2. Sandwich the back, batting and quilt top. Baste the layers together. You can create original quilting designs, or try these ideas. Quilt the center in a 4" grid. Outline the lanterns (a) and fill in the background with loops (b). Starting in the center of the freedom blocks, quilt curving lines that spiral from the center of each log to the outside of the block (c).

3. Bind the tablecloth with the 2" light blue fabric strips. Refer to Basic Techniques: Binding and Mitering Outside Corners.

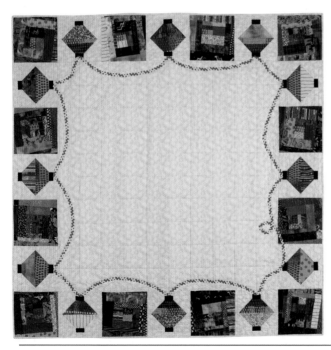

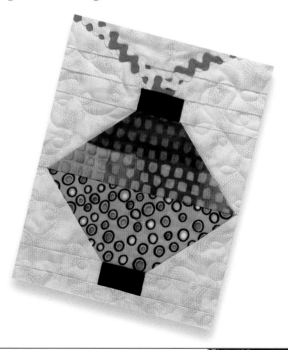

Patio Party Place Mats

Materials

Fabric (2 place mats)

½ yd. assorted medium-colored fabrics, or scrap strips left from previous projects (freedom blocks)

⅜ yd. multicolored geometric check (place mat body, freedom blocks)

¼ yd. multicolored small check (binding, freedom blocks)

¼ yd. light blue (background, binding)

⅛ yd. assorted scraps, 3" or larger, or half-square triangles left from Patio Party Quilted Tablecloth (borders)

½ yd. backing fabric

Other Supplies

2 pieces, 15" x 20", low-loft batting

6" square ruler for trimming blocks

General sewing tools and supplies

Finished size: 13" x 18½"; set of two.

Set the table for yourself and a special friend with these fun and easy Patio Party Place Mats that echo the theme of the Patio Party Wall Quilt and Quilted Tablecloth. You can use half-square triangles left from making the tablecloth to decorate the edges of the place mats. You're half done, and you haven't even started yet!

Cut

FABRIC	CUT	FOR
Assorted medium	As needed, strips 1¼" to 2¼" wide	Freedom blocks
Multicolored geometric check	2 squares, 11½" x 11½"	Place mat body
Multicolored small check	2 strips, 2" x width of fabric	Binding
Light blue	1 strip, 2" x width of fabric	Binding
	2 rectangles, 2" x 4"	Border
	4 rectangles, 2" x 3½"	Border
	2 squares, 2" x 2"	Border
	*12 squares, 2⅞" x 2⅞"	*Half-square triangles
Assorted scraps	*12 squares, 2⅞" x 2⅞"	*Half-square triangles
	Remainder, strips 1¼" and 2¼"	Freedom blocks
Backing fabric	2 rectangles, 15" x 20"	Backing

Note: If you are using half-square triangles left from the Patio Party Quilted Tablecloth project, you won't need to cut these pieces.

Construct

1. Freedom Blocks: Refer to Basic Techniques for general block construction. For this project, construct four blocks that measure approximately 7" to 8" square before trimming. Trim the blocks to 6"; skew two left and two right.

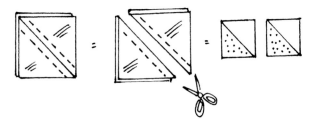

2. Half-Square Triangles: Draw a diagonal line from corner to corner on the wrong side of the 12 light blue background squares. With right sides together, match the background squares to 12 scrap squares. Stitch ¼" from each side of the line. Cut on the line. Press the seam allowance toward the scrap fabric. Make 24 half-square triangles that measure 2" x 2". If you are using half-square triangles left from the Patio Party Quilted Tablecloth, trim them to 2" x 2".

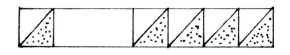

3. Side Border: Stitch a half-square triangle, a 2" x 4" background rectangle and four half-square triangles. Make two side borders.

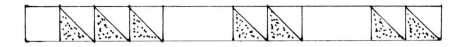

4. **Top Border:** Stitch a 2" x 2" square, three half-square triangles, a 2" x 3½" rectangle, two half-square triangles, a 2" x 3½" rectangle and two half-square triangles. Make two top borders.

Assemble and Finish

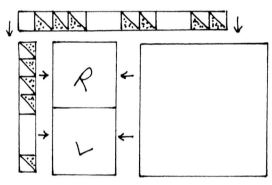

1. Stitch a left freedom block to a right freedom block. Press. Stitch the side border to the left side of the joined freedom blocks. Stitch the place mat body to the right side of the joined freedom blocks. Press. Stitch the top border to the place mat. Press. Make two place mats.

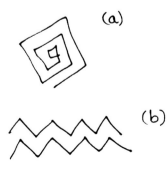

(a)

(b)

2. Layer the top and batting over the backing. Pin the layers together. Quilt the place mats.

Stitch in the ditch (on the seam line) between the freedom blocks and the place mat body and between the borders and the main body. On the freedom blocks, start at the center and quilt through each freedom block (a). On the place mat body, stitch large, free-motion zigzags (b). Outline quilt the borders.

3. Bind the left-side and top edges with the background binding strip. Bind the right-side and bottom edges with the multicolored small check binding strip. Refer to Basic Techniques: Using Two Fabrics With Overlapping Corners.

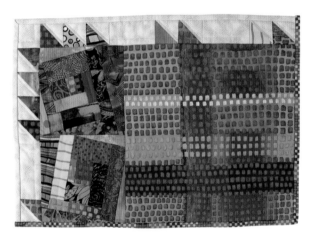

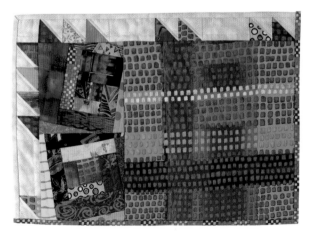

log cabin quilts with attitude

Patio Party Snack Mats

Materials

Fabric (4 snack mats)

½ yd. assorted medium-colored fabrics, or scrap strips left from previous projects (freedom blocks)

¼ yd. coordinating backing fabric

Other Supplies:

4 scraps low-loft batting, each at least 7" x 7"

6" square ruler for trimming blocks

General sewing tools and supplies

Finished size: Approximately 7" x 7", including points; part of a set of four.

These perky little mats will delight your guests. Who can resist toying with those folded points as you laugh and chat? They are just right to use for a light snack or as a coaster for your favorite drink. These snack mats are easy to finish and a perfect way to use your excess fabric from the larger projects.

Cut

FABRIC	CUT	FOR
Assorted medium or scrap strips	As needed, strips 1¼" to 2¼" wide	Freedom blocks
	16 rectangles 2¼" x 4"	Folded points
Backing	4 squares, 6" x 6"	Backing
Batting	4 squares, 7" x 7"	Batting

Construct

Folded Points
Make 16 points

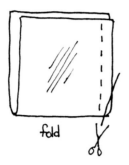

1. Fold a 2¼" x 4" rectangle in half, right sides together, to measure 2¼" x 2". Start at the fold and stitch one edge to the open end. Carefully trim the corner of the seam allowance on the folded end.

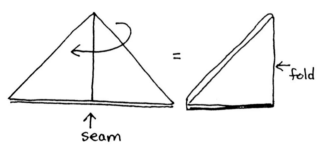

2. Turn the piece right side out. Shape it into a triangle by centering the seam; the square corner of a ruler works well to push the point into the correct shape. Press. Fold the triangle in half with the seam on the inside of the fold. Keep the raw edges even.

Freedom Blocks
Make 4 blocks

1. Refer to Basic Techniques for general block construction instructions. For this project, construct blocks approximately 7" to 8" square before trimming. Trim the blocks to 6"; skew two left and two right.

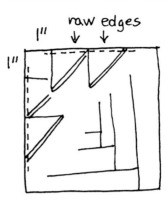

2. Pin two folded points per side to two adjacent sides of each of the four freedom blocks. Keep the raw edges of the points on the outside raw edge of the block. Pin the points 1" from the corner. Machine baste the points in place by stitching ⅛" from the raw edges.

Assemble and Finish

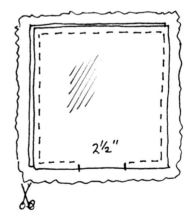

1. With right sides together, layer the backing and freedom block over the batting. Stitch ¼" from the fabric edge. Leave a 2½" opening on one side to turn the piece. Carefully trim batting from the seam allowance, trimming as close as possible without cutting the stitching. Turn the snack mat to the right side. Press lightly.

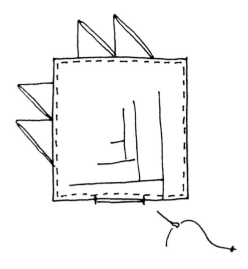

2. Hand stitch the snack mat to close the opening. Quilt the snack mats. In the mats shown, the quilting started at the center of the freedom block and went through each strip. Edgestitch to finish the mat.

Day Away Mat

Materials

Fabric

1 yd. assorted light-, medium- and dark-colored fabrics, cut into strips of varying widths between 1¼" and 2½" (freedom blocks)

¾ yd. blue (arc blocks, plain blocks, freedom blocks, binding)

⅔ yd. lime green (arc blocks, plain blocks, freedom blocks)

⅔ yd. turquoise dots (arc blocks, plain blocks, freedom blocks)

½ yd. lime dots (arc blocks, plain blocks, freedom blocks, spacers)

½ yd. stripe (arc blocks, plain blocks, freedom blocks, spacers)

½ yd. large circle print (arc blocks, freedom blocks, spacers)

¼ yd. small circle print (arc blocks, freedom blocks, spacers)

2 yd. backing fabric, striped medium-colored fabric that coordinates with top fabrics (backing, carrying strap, closures)

Other Supplies

36" x 72" batting

3" x 36" fusible batting

Matching thread (edgestitching carrying strap and closures)

12" square ruler for trimming blocks

6" hook and loop tape

General sewing tools and supplies

Inner Arc, Outer Arc and Corner Templates, pages 120 & 121

Finished size: 34" x 70".

There are days when the stress mounts and the world overwhelms you. That's the time to grab your Day Away Mat, pack up your Day Away Tote (also shown at left) and retreat to your favorite relaxing destination. This journey may take you to a tropical beach, a fantastic spa or no further than your yoga class or the corner park to meditate or enjoy a new book. Relax and enjoy your Day Away.

 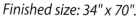

Cut

FABRIC	CUT	FOR
Assorted light, medium and dark	As needed, strips 1¼" to 2½" wide	Freedom blocks
Blue	1 rectangle, 10½" x 10½"	Plain blocks
	1 rectangle, 9½" x 17½"	Plain blocks
	1 inner arc, using template A	Arc blocks
	1 outer arc, using template B	Arc blocks
	3 corners (1 regular, 2 reversed) using template C	Arc blocks
	Remainder, strips 1¼" to 2½" wide	Freedom blocks
Lime green	1 rectangle, 8½" x 10½"	Plain blocks
	1 inner arc using template A	Arc blocks
	3 outer arcs using template B	Arc blocks
	2 corners (1 regular, 1 reversed) using template C	Arc blocks
	Remainder, strips 1¼" to 2½" wide	Freedom blocks
Turquoise dots	1 rectangle, 7½" x 10½"	Plain blocks
	1 rectangle, 8½" x 17½"	Plain blocks
	1 inner arc using template A	Arc blocks
	4 outer arcs using template B	Arc blocks
	1 corner (reversed) using template C	Arc blocks
	Remainder, strips 1¼" to 2½" wide	Freedom blocks
Lime dot	1 rectangle, 10½" x 17½"	Plain blocks
	1 inner arc using template A	Arc blocks
	2 corners using template C	Arc blocks
	1 rectangle, 2½" x 7½"	Spacer
	Remainder, strips 1¼" to 2½" wide	Freedom blocks
Stripe	1 rectangle, 9½" x 10½"	Plain blocks
	1 rectangle, 7½" x 17½"	Plain blocks
	2 inner arcs using template A	Arc blocks
	2 corners (1 regular, 1 reversed) using template C	Arc blocks
	1 rectangle, 3½" x 7½"	Spacer
	1 rectangle, 1½" x 7½"	Spacer
	Remainder, strips 1¼" to 2½" wide	Freedom blocks
Large circle print	1 inner arc using template A	Arc blocks
	5 corners (2 regular, 3 reversed) using template C	Arc blocks
	1 rectangle, 1½" x 7½"	Spacer
	Remainder, strips 1¼" to 2½" wide	Freedom blocks

FABRIC	CUT	FOR
Small circle print	1 inner arc using template A	Arc blocks
	1 corner using template C	Arc blocks
	1 rectangle, 3½" x 7½"	Spacer
	1 rectangle, 2½" x 7½"	Spacer
Backing	1 rectangle, 35" x 72"	Backing
	1 rectangle, 6" x 36"	Carrying strap
	4 rectangles, 3" x 16½"	Closures

Construct

Pieced Arc Blocks
Make 8 blocks

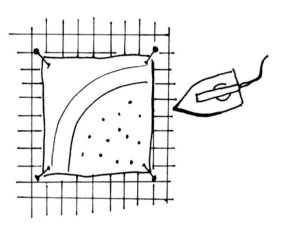

1. Clip the concave (inner) curved edge of the outer arc with tiny ⅛" clips. Match the center and quarter marks; stitch the inner and outer arcs. Check the photo for color placement. The clips will open the curve slightly to allow a smooth fit.

3. Press the blocks. The blocks can be distorted during pressing. To prevent this, draw a 7½" square on a scrap of muslin and press on the muslin, gently shaping the block to the correct size.

Freedom Blocks
Make 12 blocks

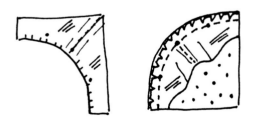

2. Join the two corner sections. Press the seam open. Clip the curved edge with tiny ⅛" clips. Matching the center and quarter marks, stitch the pieced corner to the arcs.

1. Refer to Basic Techniques for instructions on general block construction and cutting rectangular blocks. For this project, cut to the following sizes and tilts:

Row A: Cut three blocks, 9½" x 10½"; skew two right and one left.

Row B: Cut three blocks, 7½" x 9½"; skew two left and one right.

Row C: Cut three blocks, 9½" x 9½"; skew two right and one left.

Row D: Cut three blocks, 8½" x 9½"; skew two left and one right.

Assemble

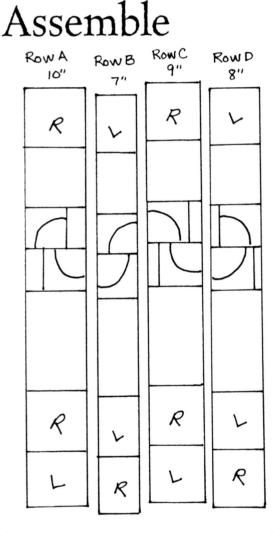

I. Lay out the quilt in vertical rows as follows:

Row A (10" wide): Right freedom block, 10" blue block, arc block with 3" spacer, 3" spacer with arc block, 17" lime dot block, right freedom block, left freedom block.

Row B (7" wide): Left freedom block, 10" turquoise dot block, arc block, arc block, 17" stripe block, left freedom block, right freedom block.

Row C (9" wide): Right freedom block, 10" stripe block, arc block with 2" spacer, 2" spacer with arc block, 17" blue block, right freedom block, left freedom block.

Row D (8" wide): Left freedom block, 10" lime block, 1" spacer with arc block, arc block with 1" spacer, 17" turquoise dot block, left freedom block, right freedom block.

2. Stitch the rows. Stitch Row A to Row B, dropping Row B by ¾". Stitch Row B to Row C, raising Row C by 1¼". Stitch Row C to Row D, dropping Row D by ¾".

Finish

Quilting and Binding

I. Lay out the quilt batting on a table. Tape the batting to the table so it is taut, but not stretched. With right sides together, lay the quilt backing and quilt top on the batting. Pin the layers in place.

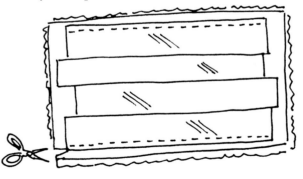

2. Stitch the two long sides. Trim the batting close to the seam line. Avoid cutting the top and backing. Turn the piece right side out, and lightly press along the seam.

3. Quilt the long vertical rows from open end to open end.

4. Bind the ends. For additional instructions, refer to Basic Techniques: Binding and Mitering Outside Corners and Binding and Mitering Inside Corners.

Carrying Strap

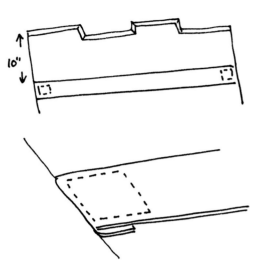

3. Stitch the strap to the back of quilt 10" down from the top, tucking under the raw edges on the ends of the strap.

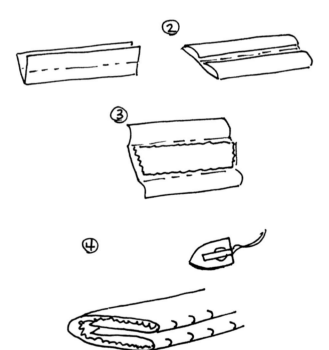

Closures

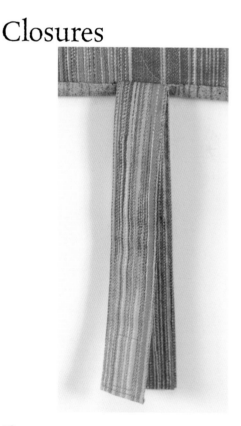

1. Press the 6" x 36" rectangle in half lengthwise, wrong sides together. Press the raw edges in toward the center. Open and center a 3" x 33½" piece of fusible quilt batting inside the strip. Refold and press again, fusing the batting in place.

2. Edgestitch both long edges of the strap.

1. Press each of the four 3" x 16½" rectangles in half lengthwise, wrong sides together. Open each rectangle. Press under ¼" of fabric on each edge of each rectangle. Close each rectangle and re-press.

2. Edgestitch the sides and ends of the straps.

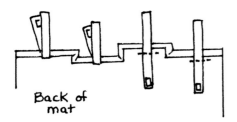

3. Stitch a 1½"-long piece of hook and loop tape to each end of each strap. Stitch the hooks on one end and loops on the reverse side of other end.

Back of mat

4. Locate the center of each strap. Pin this point to the binding on the mat back, centering one strap on each vertical row. Stitch in the ditch (right on the seam line between binding and quilt top) to secure the straps to the quilt.

5. Roll and go.

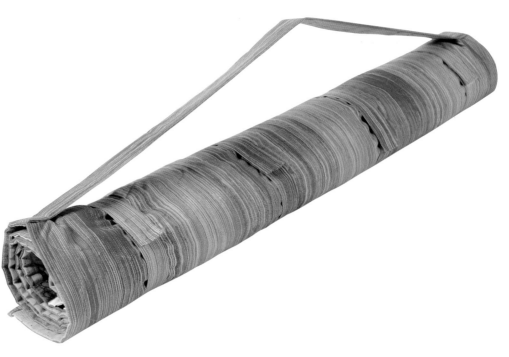

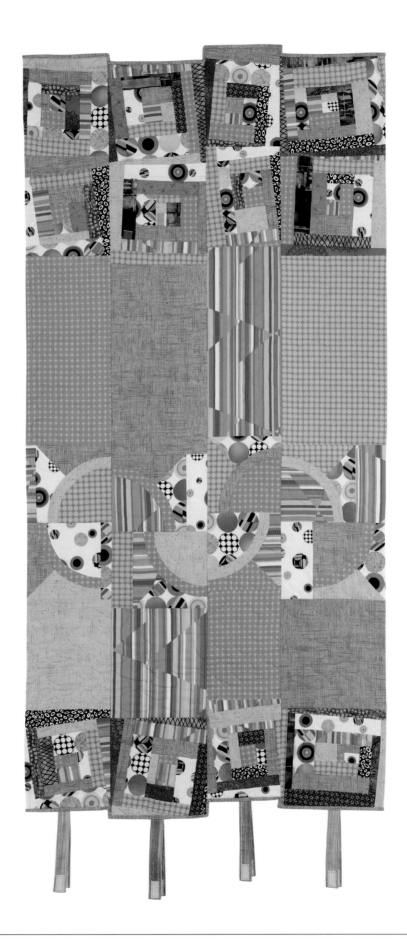

Day Away Tote

Materials

Fabric

½ yd. stripe (top of tote)

½ yd. blue (handles and trim)

1 fat quarter circle print (bottom of tote)

1 fat quarter turquoise dot (outside pocket)

1 yd. coordinating lining

Other Supplies

3 yd. blue nylon strapping, 1" wide (handles)

1 yd. clear, iron-on vinyl (bottom of tote)

12" elastic, ⅜" wide (outside pocket)

5" hook and loop closure, ¾" wide (inside pocket)

Fusible batting, 36" x 45"

Matching thread (edgestitching handles and trim)

General sewing tools and supplies

Finished size: 14" x 13" x 6".

When you escape from the pressures of life, pack the Day Away Tote with the things you enjoy, then steal away to relax and do things just for you. This roomy tote features sturdy straps and a vinyl-covered bottom. An outside pocket is perfect for your water bottle, and an inside closed pocket keeps your keys and other valuables organized. Run fast, and enjoy your day away.

Cut

FABRIC	CUT	FOR
Stripe	2 rectangles, 12" x 20"	Tote top
Blue	2 strips, 2" x 20"	Trim
	2 strips, 3¼" x 45½"; piece to get the needed length	Handles
Circle print	1 rectangle, 15" x 20"	Tote bottom
Turquoise dot	1 rectangle, 10½" x 16"	Outside pocket
Lining	1 rectangle, 22" x 40"	Tote body
	1 rectangle, 8" x 28"	Inside pocket
	2 strips, 1¾" x 20"	Top edge of tote
Batting	1 rectangle, 22" x 40"	Tote body
	1 strip, 1½" x 45"	Handles
	1 rectangle, 7½" x 10½"	Outside pocket

Construct

Handles

Make 2

1. Press the raw lengthwise edges of a 3¼" x 45½" strip, wrong sides together, to the center of the strip. Open the strip, and center a 1½" x 45" strip of fusible batting on the strip. Refold. Press to fuse the batting inside the handle.

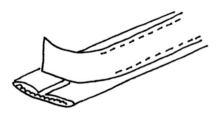

2. Cover the raw edges with 1"-wide nylon strapping. Stitch both sides. Make two handles.

Outside Pocket

1. Fold the 10½" x 16" rectangle in half, wrong sides together, so it measures 8" x 10½". Stitch an elastic casing ½" from the folded edge.

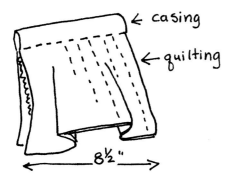

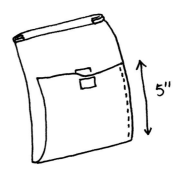

2. Cut a piece of fusible batting 7½" x 10½", and fuse it between the layers. Quilt vertical lines up to, but not through, the casing. Make two small pleats at the bottom edge, so the pocket measures 8½" wide.

2. Turn up the bottom folded edge by 5". Center the hook and loop tape on the pocket; stitch it in place. Edgestitch the sides of the pocket.

Assemble and Finish

3. Insert the elastic. Stitch one end of elastic in place, and tighten the elastic to measure 8". Stitch the elastic to hold it in place, and trim the excess.

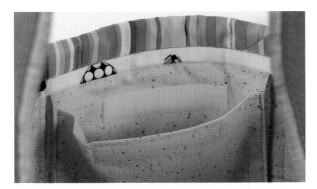

Inside Pocket

1. Follow the manufacturer's directions to attach the clear, iron-on vinyl to the right side of the tote bottom. Save the vinyl pressing paper to protect the vinyl as you press the tote.

1. With right sides together, fold the inside pocket to measure 8" x 14". Stitch the side seams. Turn the pocket to the right side, and press.

2. Fold the blue trim strips in half lengthwise, wrong sides together, and press.

3. With the raw edges even, layer one tote top (right side down), the vinyl-covered tote bottom (right side up) and the folded trim strip. Stitch a ¼" seam. Repeat on the other end of bag. Your seams will be on the right side of the bag. Lightly press open.

4. Layer the lining, fusible batting and tote exterior. Quilt 2" horizontal lines on the tote bottom, and quilt randomly spaced vertical lines on the tote top. Trim the excess lining and batting.

5. Center the elastic pocket on the bag front. The bottom raw edges of the pocket should touch the seam allowance. Pin the pocket in place.

6. Center the handles on the center front, approximately 8" apart and 4½" from the side edge. The bottom raw edges should touch the seam allowance, and the handles should cover the side raw edges of the pocket. Pin in place.

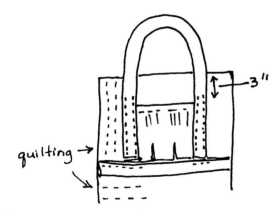

7. Edgestitch both sides of the handles, starting at the bottom raw edges and stopping 3" from the top edge of the tote. Backstitch to secure . Make sure that you catch in the sides of the pocket.

8. Press the folded trim toward the tote top. Press only the trim. Protect the vinyl with the vinyl pressing paper, and avoid pressing on the vinyl.

9. Edgestitch the top folded edge of the trim, catching in the raw ends of the handles and the bottom of the pocket.

10. Add the handles to the tote back, and stitch the trim.

11. Finish the top edge of the tote. With right sides together, match one long edge of a 1¾" x 20" strip to the top exterior raw edges of the tote. Stitch ¼" from the edge. Turn to the back side, and stitch in the ditch to encase the raw edges.

12. With right sides together, pin the sides of the tote, matching the trim. Don't pin the vinyl. Stitch the sides of the tote. Neaten the raw edges with serging, zigzagging or encasing.

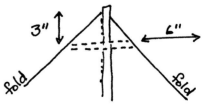

13. Miter the bottom of the tote. On the inside of the tote, match the side seam with the center of the bottom to form a triangle. Mark 3" down from the point of the triangle. Draw a line perpendicular to the seam. This will be 6" long, and it will start and end on quilting lines. Stitch the miter, and reinforce it with a second row of stitching ⅛" away. There is no need to trim off the triangle; it will help to stabilize the tote bottom.

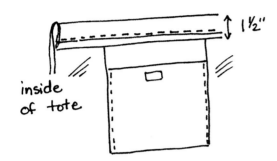

14. Pin the raw edges of the inside pocket to the back lining, 1½" down from the top and centered between the handles. Press the top of the tote to the inside to form a 1½" hem. Stitch the top hem; catch the inside pocket in your stitching, but avoid catching the handles.

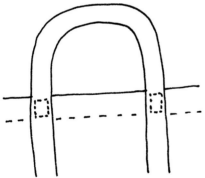

15. Turn up the handles and reinforce them to the top of the tote by stitching a rectangle through the handle, tote and tote hem.

Variation
Designer Finish for a Ready-Made Tote

Add a personal touch to a ready-made canvas bag, or bring new life to a usable but outdated tote with this designer finish.

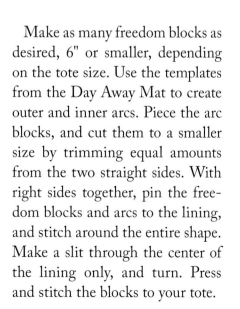

Make as many freedom blocks as desired, 6" or smaller, depending on the tote size. Use the templates from the Day Away Mat to create outer and inner arcs. Piece the arc blocks, and cut them to a smaller size by trimming equal amounts from the two straight sides. With right sides together, pin the freedom blocks and arcs to the lining, and stitch around the entire shape. Make a slit through the center of the lining only, and turn. Press and stitch the blocks to your tote.

Let the Seeds Fall Where They May Quilt

Materials

Fabric

6¾ yd. assorted florals, prints and solids (freedom blocks)

3 yd. pale green (appliqué background)

¾ yd. green leaf print (binding)

¾ yd. medium green print (vines)

4 fat quarters green prints or solids (leaves and sepals)

3 fat quarters purple prints (flowers)

3 fat quarters orange or pink prints (flowers)

9 yd. backing

Other Supplies

96" x 108" cotton batting

4 yd. paper-backed fusible adhesive

4 yd. orange medium or small rickrack (flowers)

2½ yd. green medium rickrack (leaves)

2 yd. tan medium rickrack (leaves)

2 yd. brown medium rickrack (leaves)

1½ yd. yellow medium rickrack (flowers)

Decorative threads for appliqué

9½" or 12" square ruler for trimming blocks

General sewing tools and supplies

Let the Seeds Fall Where They May Templates on Pages 122 & 123

Finished size: 90" x 100".

Awaken to a bright, new day under this lively collection of colors and patterns. You'll love the combination of freedom blocks with appliqué that make this beautiful queen-size strippy quilt. Pieced leaves can be made with ease. Fuse them in place before permanently attaching your leaves with decorative machine stitching. Finish the quilt by adding colorful blooms complete with rickrack trim.

Cut

FABRIC	CUT	FOR
Assorted florals, prints and solids	As needed, strips 1¼" to 3" wide	Freedom blocks
Pale green	1 strip, 18½" x 104"	Center applique panel
	2 strips, 9½" x 104"	Side applique panels
Green leaf print	10 strips, 2" x width of fabric; piece to total 385"	Binding
Medium green print	1"-wide bias strips; piece to make: • 3 vines, 1" x 64" • 2 vines, 1" x 55" • 2 vines, 1" x 45" • Short vines, 4" to 6" long, totaling 124"	Center panel Side panels Side panels Center and side panels
Green, purple, orange and pink prints	Appliqué shapes, as directed, using templates on pages 122 and 123	Leaf and flower appliqués

Construct

Let the Seeds Fall Where They May Quilt Side Panel Leaf and Flower Placement

Let the Seeds Fall Where They May Quilt Center Panel Leaf and Flower Placement

Let the Seeds Fall Where
They May Quilt
Center Appliqué Panel
Total length of design: 83"

Let the Seeds Fall Where
They May Quilt
Side Appliqué Panel
Total length of design: 54"

Vines

1. Press the vines in half lengthwise, with the wrong sides together. Press the vines in half lengthwise again, covering the raw edges with the folded edge, to create ¼"-wide stem. Press well; a little spray starch may help.

2. Open the last fold so the stem measures ½" wide. Pin it on the appliqué panels. Use the diagram for the placement of vines and flowers. You may want to prepare the leaves and flowers first to help in the layout and placement of the vines. After placing the vines, remove the leaves and flowers, and complete the vines first. Tuck the ends of the short vines under the longer vines to conceal the raw edges. Finish stitching (Steps 3 and 4) the short vines before stitching the long vines.

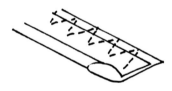

3. Use a small zigzag stitch (2.0 width x 2.0 length) to stitch the raw edge onto the background.

4. Refold the folded edge over the raw edge. Topstitch the vine down, covering the raw edges. You can use a small decorative stitch or a small zigzag stitch. I used a diagonal zigzag stitch with a variegated rayon thread for the quilt pictured.

Pieced Leaves

Leaf A
Make 4

1. Stack two sets of three assorted green print fabrics, right sides up. Cut the stacks approximately 1" larger than the leaf shape. Look at the pattern for a guide, and make two freehand cuts, dividing the leaf into three sections.

2. Rearrange the fabrics within each set to make different combinations, and stitch them together with a narrow seam. Ignore the fact that you have added no seam allowance. Press flat. Make four leaves. I made the two remaining leaves and saved them for the Let the Seeds Fall Where They May Runner.

3. Reverse the leaf pattern, and draw the outside shape of the leaf onto the paper side of the fusible adhesive web. Rough cut the fusible web ¼" larger than the outside of the leaf. Cut ¼" inside the drawn line, leaving a "skeleton" of fusible web. This ½" skeleton will be enough to bond the fabric to the background, yet leave the appliqué flexible enough to avoid a stiff, fused-on look.

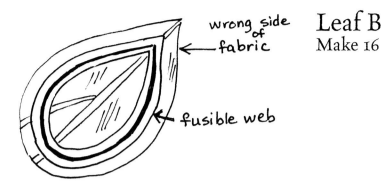

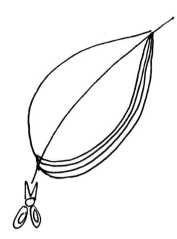

Leaf B
Make 16

4. Press the skeleton of fusible web to the wrong side of the pieced leaf. Center the seam at the tip of the leaf. Trim the outside of the leaf to the drawn line. Remove the paper backing.

1. Stack four sets of four assorted green fabrics, right sides up. Cut the stacks approximately 1" larger than the Leaf B shape. Use the pattern as a guide, and cut the leaf into two sections as shown.

2. Rearrange the fabrics within each set to make different combinations. Stitch them together with a narrow seam. Ignore the fact that you have added no seam allowance. Press flat. Make 16 leaves — eight for the center panel and four for each side panel.

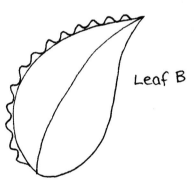

Leaf B

5. Position a Leaf A on each of the ends of the vines that are stitched to the center appliqué panel. Tuck green medium rickrack behind one side of the leaf, exposing half of the rickrack along the leaf edge. Hide the ends of the rickrack under the leaf. Press to bond the leaf and rickrack in place.

6. Appliqué around the leaves. For the quilt shown, I used a blanket stitch (1.5 length and 2.0 width) with a rayon decorative thread. To secure the threads, pull the ends to the wrong side and tie.

3. Continue to make and apply the fusible adhesive "skeletons" as you did for Leaf A. Position the leaves on the appliqué panels. Add green or brown medium rickrack, fuse, and stitch in place.

Leaf C
Make 6

1. Stack three sets of two green fabrics, right sides up. Make Leaf C following the same general instructions as for Leaf B. Make six leaves, two for each panel.

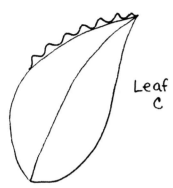

Leaf C

2. Add rickrack trim only halfway down one side of Leaf C.

Leaf D
Make 32

1. Trace the pattern onto the paper side of the fusible web. Cut "skeletons," and fuse them onto the wrong side of the green fabrics. Make 18 for the center appliqué panel and seven for each side appliqué panel.

2. Trim the pieces to leaf shape, and place them on the panels. Fuse and appliqué the leaves. Leaf D does not have rickrack trim.

Flowers

Flower A
Make 8

1. Reverse the flower pattern, and trace it onto the paper side of your fusible web. Separate the petals. Trace them as three parts; add a narrow underlap on Petals 1 and 2.

2. Following the instructions for Leaf A, cut the "skeletons" and fuse them onto the wrong side of the purple flower fabrics. Trim the pieces to the correct size.

Flower A*

3. Remove the paper backing and position the pieces on the appliqué panels. Fuse Petal 1 in place. Add yellow medium rickrack trim behind Petals 2 and 3, and fuse in place. Appliqué the flowers, pull the ends of the threads to the back, and tie the threads.

Flowers B, C and D
Make 8 Flower B, 16 Flower C and 14 Flower D

1. Reverse the flower patterns and trace them onto the fusible web. Cut the "skeletons." Because some areas of these flowers are narrow, you will be able to remove only small sections of the web.

2. Fuse the web pattern pieces to the wrong side of the flower fabrics. Flowers B and C are orange or pink. Flower D is purple. Trim the pieces.

3. Position the pieces on the panels. Add orange rickrack to Flowers B and C and yellow rickrack to Flower D. Fuse and appliqué the flowers in place.

Row 1	Row 2	Row 3	Row 4	Row 5	Row 6
L	R	L	R	L	R
R	L	R	L	R	L
L	R	L	R	L	R
R	L	R	L	R	L
L	R	L	R	L	R
R	L	R	L	R	L
L	R	L	R	L	R
R	L	R	L	R	L
L	R	L	R	L	R
R	L	R	L	R	L
L	R	L	R	L	R

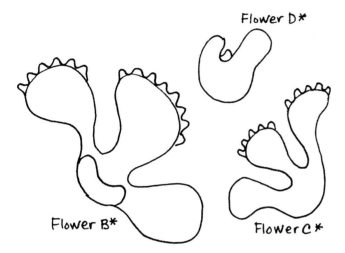

Flower D*

Flower B*

Flower C*

4. Add the green sepals to Flower B.

Freedom Blocks

1. Construct 66 freedom blocks that measure approximately 10" to 12" square before trimming. Trim the blocks to 9½" x 9½". Skew 33 left and 33 right. Refer to Basic Techniques for general block instructions.

2. Arrange the freedom blocks in vertical rows of 11 blocks each.

Rows 1, 3 and 5: Start with a left block, alternate with a right block, and repeat the pattern for the rest of the row.

Rows 2, 4 and 6: Start with a right block, alternate with a left block, and repeat the pattern for the rest of the row.

3. Stitch Row 2 to Row 3. Stitch Row 4 to Row 5. Press.

Assemble

1. Lay out strips of pieced blocks and the appliqué panels as indicated.

2. Center the appliqué panels. Trim the top and bottom ends to fit the size of the pieced blocks. Stitch the rows together to complete the top.

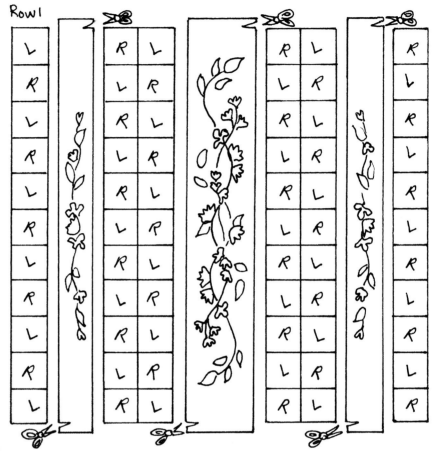

Finish

1. Piece the backing, and trim it to 94" x 104".

2. Layer the quilt, and baste it. Choose your own quilting patterns, or try this plan. In the freedom strips, machine quilt a cable design. In the appliqué panels, hand or machine quilt around each shape, and add a diamond design in the background.

3. Bind the quilt with the 2"-wide green leaf print strips. Refer to Basic Techniques: Mitering and Binding Outside Corners for additional instructions.

Let the Seeds Fall Where They May Runner

Materials

Fabric

2 yd. pale green (appliqué background, folded trim and quilt back)

½ yd. medium-dark green (vines)

½ yd. medium green print (binding)

4 fat quarters green prints (leaves)

3 fat eighths purple prints (flowers)

3 fat eighths orange prints (flowers)

Other Supplies

22" x 66" lightweight batting

2 yd. paper-backed fusible adhesive web

1 yd. of green medium rickrack (leaves)

1 yd. orange medium or
small rickrack (flowers)

1 yd. brown medium rickrack (leaves)

½ yd. yellow medium rickrack (flowers)

Decorative threads for appliqué

General sewing tools and supplies

Let the Seeds Fall Where They May
Templates on Pages 122 & 123

Finished size: 18" x 62".

The Let the Seeds Fall Where They May Runner is as delightful and carefree as the coordinating quilt. With a whimsical scattering of flowers, this versatile piece provides the perfect way to complete your bedroom. Hang it vertically in your adjoining bathroom. Use it on the bed to cover your pillows, serve as a headboard, or complement the area above the headboard of your bed. Or, put it to another use to cover a dresser, chest or bench. The decorating options are endless. The instructions offer two options for the background — pieced or whole-cloth. Pick the one that matches your style the best.

Cut

FABRIC	CUT	FOR
Pale green, Option 1: pieced background	1 rectangle, 18" x 35"	Center appliqué panel
	2 rectangles, 14" x 18"	Side appliqué panels
	2 strips, 2" x 18"	Folded trim
	1 rectangle, 21" x 65"	Backing
Pale green, Option 2: whole-cloth background	1 rectangle, 18" x 62"	Appliqué panel
	1 rectangle, 21" x 65"	Backing
Medium green print	5 strips, 2" x width of fabric; piece to make 166"	Binding
Medium-dark green	1"-wide bias strips; piece to make: • 2 strips, 1" x 46" • Short strips, 4" to 6", totaling 50"	Vines Vines
Green prints, purple prints and orange prints	Appliqué shapes, as directed, using templates on pages 122 and 123	Flower and leaf appliques

Construct

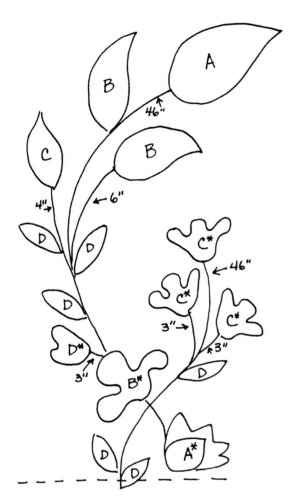

Let the Seeds Fall Where They May
Runner Section Layout Diagram

Let the Seeds Fall Where They
May Runner Layout Diagram
Total length of design: 54"

Appliqué Panel

Option 1 (Pieced Background)

1. Press the two 2" x 18" trim strips in half lengthwise, wrong sides together, to make two 1"-wide strips. Baste one strip to each end of the 18" x 35" rectangle; match the raw edges. Attach a 14" side panel to each end of the center, and stitch the folded trim in the seam. Press the trim toward the side panels.

Option 2 (Whole-Cloth Background)

1. Proceed to the next step.

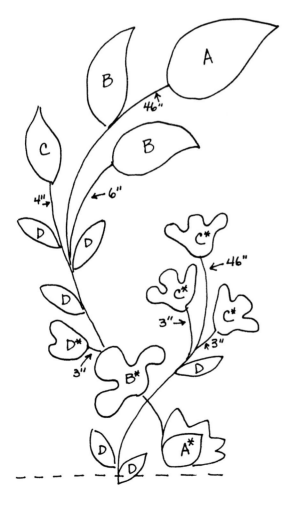

Vines

1. Make the vines. Refer to the instructions for the Let the Seeds Fall Where They May Quilt.

2. Place the vines. Refer to the placement diagram for the Let the Seeds Fall Where They May Runner.

Pieced Leaves

Leaf A
Make 2, or use leaves left from the Let the Seeds Fall Where They May Quilt

1. Cut one set of three green fabrics that are approximately 1" larger than the leaf shape. Stack and cut the shapes twice, curving the cut diagonally from corner to corner. Continue following the instructions for the Let the Seeds Fall Where They May Quilt.

2. Place the leaves. Refer to the diagram for the Let the Seeds Fall Where They May Runner for placement.

Leaf B
Make 4

1. Cut two sets of two green fabrics that are approximately 1" larger than the leaf shape. Stack the shapes and cut them once, curving the cut diagonally from corner to corner. Continue following the instructions for the Let the Seeds Fall Where They May Quilt.

2. Place the leaves. Refer to the placement diagram for the Let the Seeds Fall Where They May Runner.

Leaf C
Make 2

1. Cut two green fabrics that are roughly 1" larger than the leaf shape. Stack and cut the shapes once, curving the cut diagonally from corner to corner. Continue making the leaf. Add rickrack trim halfway down one side of each Leaf C.

2. Place the leaves. Refer to the diagram for the Let the Seeds Fall Where They May Runner for placement.

Leaf D
Make 12

1. Trace the leaf pattern on fusible web. Cut the fusible web "skeleton," and fuse it on the wrong side of the green fabric.

2. Trim and position the leaves on the panel. Refer to the diagram for the Let the Seeds Fall Runner Where They May Runner for placement. Appliqué the leaves in place. Leaf D does not have rickrack trim.

Flowers
Make 2 Flower A, 2 Flower B, 6 Flower C and 2 Flower D

1. Make the flowers; refer to the instructions for the Let the Seeds Fall Where They May Quilt.

2. Place the flowers; refer to the placement diagram for the Let the Seeds Fall Where They May Runner.

Finish

1. Layer the backing, batting and quilt top. Baste. Quilt around the appliquéd shapes. Quilt a diamond grid in the background.

2. Bind the quilt with the 2" medium green strips. Refer to Basic Techniques: Mitering and Binding Outside Corners.

Flying Free Butterfly Pillow

Materials

Fabric

½ yd. of assorted floral, print and solid strips, varying between 1" to 2½" wide (freedom blocks)

½ yd. muslin (lining)

Fat quarter of coordinating print (pillow back)

Other Supplies

14" x 18" pillow form

1 yd. wire-edged ribbon (butterfly body and antennae)

½ yd. yellow jumbo rickrack (top edge of pillow)

9" or larger square ruler for trimming blocks

General sewing tools and supplies

Finished size: 12" x 16".

This enchanting pillow provides the perfect accent to the Let the Seeds Fall Where They May Quilt. You can make it easily from four freedom blocks that use scraps from your previous projects. Add jumbo-sized rickrack trim and wired ribbon to complete the pillow. It's as quick to make as it is delightful to behold.

Cut

FABRIC	CUT	FOR
Assorted florals, prints and solids	As needed, strips 1" to 2½" wide	Freedom blocks
Muslin	2 rectangles 15" x 19"	Lining
Coordinating print	1 rectangle 13" x 17"	Pillow back

Construct

Freedom Blocks

Make 4

I. Make four freedom blocks that measure approximately 10" to 11" before trimming. Trim each block to 7" x 9"; skew two left and two right. Refer to Basic Techniques for detailed block construction and cutting instructions.

2. Stitch the blocks into a four-patch as shown, alternating the left and right skewed blocks. Press.

Quilt

I. Layer a muslin lining rectangle, batting and pillow top. Pin baste the layers. Quilt a whimsical pattern, such as a butterfly that has one wing section covering each freedom block. Trim the backing and batting even with the top.

Finish

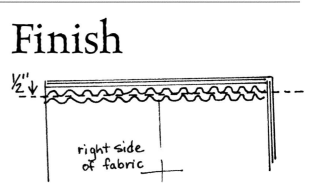

right side of fabric

I. Pin the yellow jumbo rickrack to the top edge of the pillow on the right side of the fabric. Center the rickrack ½" from the edge, and baste it in place.

2. Add a layer of lining to the pillow back. With right sides together, use a ½" seam to stitch the quilt top to the pillow back. Leave an opening on the bottom edge for turning.

3. Turn the piece right side out, and insert the pillow form. Neatly stitch the opening closed.

4. Tie wire-edged ribbon around the center of the pillow, cinching it to form the butterfly's wings. Position the ends of the ribbon at the top of the pillow. Curl the ends of ribbon to form the antennae.

Forest Floor Wall Quilt

Materials

Fabric

1 yd. assorted medium- to dark-colored fabrics (freedom blocks)

¾ yd. light gray background (inner borders 1, 4)

⅝ yd. autumn leaf print (plain blocks, freedom blocks)

½ yd. dark, small leaf print (inner border 3, binding, freedom blocks)

½ yd. or fat quarters of one or two dark brown prints (vines)

¼ yd. dark stripe (inner border 2)

⅛ yd. orange (berries)

1⅛ yd. backing

Other Supplies

38" x 38" batting

2 yd. medium rickrack in orange, burgundy or tan (berries)

½ yd. paper-backed fusible adhesive (berries)

Brown permanent fabric pen or marker (stems, tendrils)

Dark brown thread (stems, tendrils)

Orange thread (berries)

6" square ruler for trimming freedom blocks

General sewing tools and supplies

Finished size: 35" x 35".

One of the delights of autumn is rustling through the fallen leaves and viewing the rich parade of colors. Who can resist the dangling beauty of bittersweet vines that give life to an old stone wall? Bring that same splendor of autumn into your home with the Forest Floor Wall Quilt. Leaf-print fabrics give the quilt a distinctive fall flavor, while rickrack adds a three-dimensional touch to the appliquéd bittersweet vines and berries.

Cut

FABRIC	CUT	FOR
Medium to dark fabrics	As needed, strips 1¼" to 2¼" wide	Freedom blocks
Light gray	4 strips, 3" x width of fabric	Inner border 1
	4 strips, 1¾" x width of fabric	Inner border 4
Autumn leaf print	3 strips, 5½" x width of fabric, into: • 17 squares, 5½" x 5½"	Plain blocks
	Remainder, strips 1¼" to 2¼" wide	Freedom blocks
Dark small leaf print	4 strips, 2" x width of fabric	Binding
	4 strips, 1¼" x width of fabric	Inner border 3
Dark brown prints	8 strips on the bias, 1" x diagonal width of fabric (approximately 17" to 18")	Bias strips
	Remainder, strips 1¼" to 2¼" wide	Freedom blocks
Dark stripe	4 strips, 1" x width of fabric	Inner border 2
Orange	Trace 29 circles, ½" diameter, on the paper side of fusible adhesive, bond it to the wrong side of the fabric and trim to size before removing paper	Berries

Construct and Assemble

Freedom Blocks

Make 16

1. Construct 16 blocks that measure approximately 7" before trimming. Trim to 5½" x 5½". Skew eight left and eight right. Refer to Basic Techniques for general block construction information.

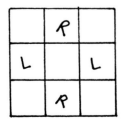

2. Lay out the quilt center as shown, using five plain blocks, two left freedom blocks and two right freedom blocks. Stitch the blocks into rows. Stitch the rows together. Press.

Inner Borders

Make 4

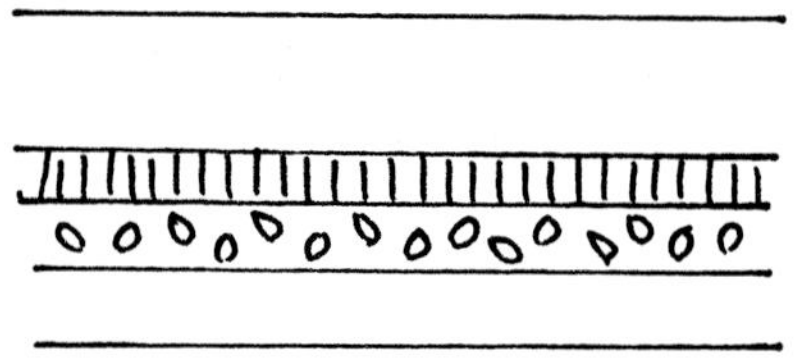

1. Stitch together a 3" background strip, 1" dark stripe strip, 1¼" dark small-leaf strip, and 1¾" background strip. Make four borders.

2. With right sides together, pin the border to the pieced quilt top; be sure to match the centers. Mark dots ¼" from the corners of the quilt top. Stitch the border to the quilt, starting and stopping at the dots. Backstitch to secure the border. Avoid allowing the backstitching to go past the marked corner dots.

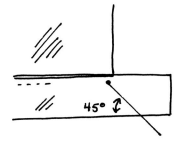

3. On the wrong side of the border, draw 45-degree lines from the marked corner dots to the outside of the border. Check that the border is getting larger as you go out from the dot.

4. Stitch the remaining borders onto the quilt top.

Bittersweet Corners Option: If you wish to make rectangular Bittersweet Corners, proceed as follows. Instead of centering the inner border strip on the quilt top, extend only 9" to 10" of the border strip on one side of the quilt top. This will leave a longer strip of border at the other end. Continue with stitching and marking the 45-degree lines.

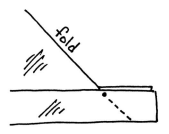

5. Align the marked corner dots and 45-degree lines on two adjacent sides of the quilt top. Stitch on the line, starting from the outer edge

and proceeding to the dot. Backstitch at the dot. Check the mitered corner to ensure that it lays flat. Trim the excess border; leave a ¼" seam allowance. Save the ends of the borders for Bittersweet Corners. Press the seam open.

6. Continue working around the quilt until you have mitered, trimmed and pressed all of the corners.

Outer Pieced Border

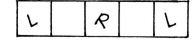

1. Stitch the side border as shown, using a left freedom block, plain block, right freedom block, plain block and left freedom block. Make two side borders. Attach one border each to opposite sides of the quilt top.

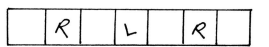

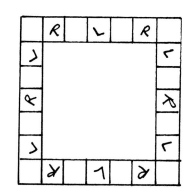

2. Stitch the top/bottom border using a plain block, right freedom block, plain block, left freedom block, plain block, right freedom block and plain block. Make two borders. Attach one border each to the top and bottom of the quilt top.

Appliqué

1. Bittersweet vines: Press the 1" dark brown bias strips in half lengthwise, wrong sides together.

2. Open a few stitches of the seam between inner border 1 and inner border 2, approximately 2" to 3" from the corner. Insert one end of the vine into the opening. Pin to curve the vines on the light gray background. Extend two vines in each direction from the corner as shown in the photo.

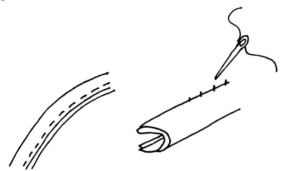

3. Stitch a scant ¼" from the raw edges of each vine to secure. Press the folded edge over to conceal the raw edges, and hand stitch it.

4. Re-stitch the seam.

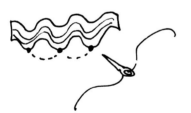

5. Cut small pieces of rickrack as shown. By hand, stitch the three points together to form three-dimensional husks for the berries.

6. Remove the paper backing from the berries, and position them on the quilt top. Before fusing them in place, add the rickrack husks behind the berry tops. Trim the rickrack ends, and tuck them under the berry. Fuse the berry.

7. Use orange thread to stitch around the berries; be sure the stitching catches the ends of the rickrack.

8. Use a brown permanent fabric pen or marker to draw stems that connect the berries to the vines.

Finish

1. Sandwich the backing, batting and quilt top. Baste the layers together. Choose your own quilting designs, or try these ideas that combine machine quilting with an accent of hand quilting. Cross hatch the blocks to create a diagonal grid. Outline quilt the inner borders and vines. Use brown thread to stitch the stems. Hand quilt random lines in the background to create a stone look.

2. Piece the 2" strips of dark, small-leaf print to make 150" of binding. Bind the quilt. Refer to Basic Techniques: Binding and Mitering Outside Corners for detailed instructions.

3. Add a rod pocket to the top of the quilt.

Bittersweet Corners

Materials

Fabric

Trimmed sections left from the Forest Floor Wall Quilt mitered corners (borders)

Bittersweet Corner No. 1: 8" x 8" square light gray (quilt center)

Bittersweet Corner No. 2: 4" x 11½" rectangle dark brown (quilt center)

⅛ yd. each of light gray, dark brown and rust (binding)

Remaining dark brown prints left from the Forest Floor Wall Quilt (vines)

Scraps of orange (berries)

½ yd. backing

Other Supplies

2 yd. medium rickrack in orange, burgundy or tan (berries)

½ yd. paper-backed fusible adhesive (berries)

30" x 30" batting, or a size appropriate for your project

Brown permanent fabric pen or marker (stems and tendrils)

Dark brown thread (stems and tendrils)

Orange thread (berries)

General sewing tools and supplies

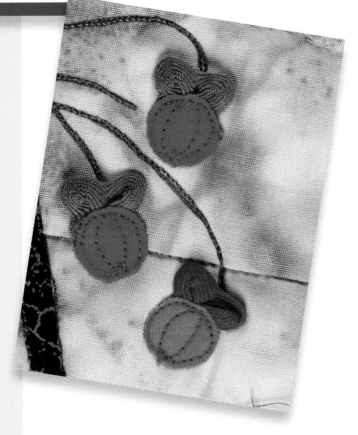

Finished sizes: 12" x 12" (No. 1), 8" x 15" (No. 2) and 10" x 19" (No. 3).

Savor every bit of breathtaking autumn-themed fabric when you cleverly turn your trimmed ends from the Forest Floor Wall Quilt into original miniature works of art. Make one or the whole grouping to add a co-ordinating accent. Grab your mitered corners and the rest of your scraps, and get started. The Bittersweet Corners shown are to provide you with inspiration. Choose how to use the leftover pieces you have to make your own unique creations.

Note: Because you are making original artworks, your fabric needs and finished results may vary from those listed and shown.

Construct and Assemble

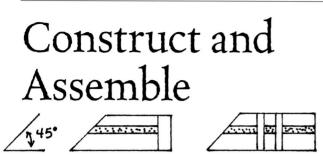

I. Choose two mitered border strips to create your miniature quilt. If the strips are of equal length, the quilt will be square, like Bittersweet Corner No. 1. If one strip is short and the other long, the quilt will be rectangular, like Bittersweet Corner No. 2. If you use two unequal sets of strips, the quilt can look like Bittersweet Corner No. 3. Any strip can be lengthened by adding to the straight end of the strip or by stashing and adding fabric into the strip.

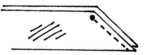

2. Check to see that all of the diagonal cuts measure 45 degrees. If not, trim the cuts to 45 degrees before joining the strips. To make the mitered corner, mark a dot ¼" from the edges as shown. Stitch on the diagonal edge to the dot, then backstitch. Press the seam open.

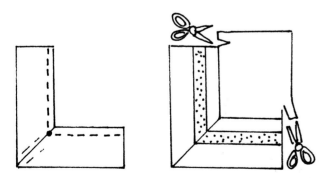

3. Mark a dot ¼" from the corner of the quilt top center. Pin the center to the mitered corner, matching the dots. Stitch to the dot, then backstitch. Repeat for the second side. Trim any excess.

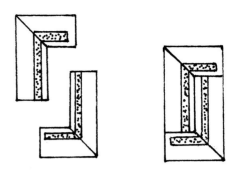

I. Make Bittersweet Corner No. 3 by using two mitered corners. After mitering the corners, cut the two corners to exactly the same size by laying one corner on top of the other. Lay the corners out as diagrammed. With right sides together, stitch the center seam from dot to dot. Backstitch at the dots. Stitch the two remaining seams, backstitching at the dots. Press.

Appliqué

I. Add the vine and berry appliqués. Refer to the directions in the Forest Floor Wall Quilt. Note that the vines are coming from the edges of the quilt, so you will not have to open any seams.

Finish

I. Quilt the Bittersweet Corners to coordinate with the Forest Floor Wall Quilt.

2. Cut two strips, 2" by the fabric width, and piece them to create binding strips. Bind the quilts. Refer to Basic Techniques: Binding and Mitering Outside Corners for detailed instructions.

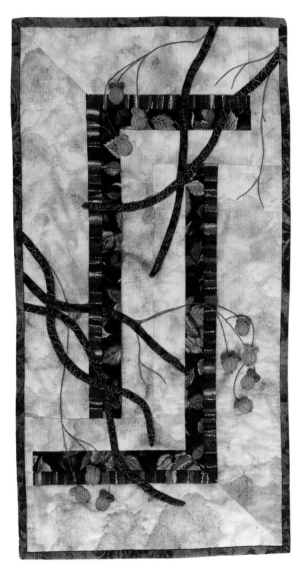

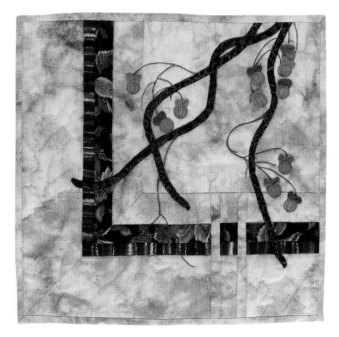

La Bohemia Wall Quilt

Materials

Fabric

2 yd. assorted brightly colored prints and solids (freedom blocks)

1½ yd. medium/dark yellow (border 4)

1 yd. medium yellow (border 2)

1 yd. red/print 1 (flowers, prairie points)

¾ yd. blue/print 1 (birds, binding)

½ yd. red/print 2 (flowers)

¼ yd. multicolored print (border 1)

1 fat quarter pale yellow (center background)

1 fat quarter solid red (flowers)

1 fat quarter blue/print 2 (leaves)

1 fat eighth blue/print 3 (corners for border 1)

3 yd. backing, or 49 squares, 8½" x 8½"

Other Supplies

7 yd. red medium rickrack (binding, flowers)

4½ yd. blue medium rickrack (border 2, birds)

3 yd. paper-backed fusible adhesive web

54" x 54" batting

Invisible thread (attaching rickrack)

Decorative thread (appliqué)

6½" or larger ruler for trimming freedom blocks

Fabric glue that dries clear

General sewing tools and supplies

La Bohemia Quilt Templates on pages 124 & 125

Finished size: 51" x 51".

Nothing tops the excitement of a folk bazaar, whether you are exploring the fascinating markets of far-off Budapest or simply absorbing the atmosphere at a local cultural festival. La Bohemia captures the colors of handcrafted tableware and linens and the movement of swirling skirts on gaily dressed dancers. Fused appliqué, rickrack trim and prairie points combine with freedom blocks to add to the charm of your La Bohemia Wall Quilt.

Cut

FROM	CUT	FOR
Assorted brightly colored prints and solids	As needed, strips 1" to 2½" wide	Freedom blocks
Medium to dark yellow	2 strips (lengthwise), 4" x 51½"	Borders
	2 strips (lengthwise), 4" x 44½"	Borders
	3 strips, 1½" x width or length, into: • 12 rectangles, 1½" x 6½"	Spacers for border 3
Medium yellow	2 strips, 5½" x fabric width, into: • 4 strips, 5½" x 20½"	Border 2
	1 strip, 5½" x fabric width, into: • 4 squares, 5½" x 5½"	Border 2
	3 strips, 1½" x fabric width, into: • 12 rectangles, 1½" x 6½"	Border 3 spacers
Red/print 1	6 strips, 3½" x width of fabric, into: • 60 squares, 3½" x 3½"	Prairie points
	4 small flowers	Border 2 appliqué
	Remainder, strips 1" to 2½" wide	Freedom blocks
Blue/print 1	6 strips, 2¼" x width of fabric; piece to needed length	Binding
	2 birds (1 regular, 1 reversed)	Center appliqué
	Remainder, strips 1" to 2½" wide	Freedom blocks
Red/print 2	2 large-sectioned flowers	Center, appliqué
	5 small flowers	Center and border 2 appliqué
	Remainder, strips 1" to 2½" wide	Freedom blocks
Multicolored print	4 rectangles, 2" x 17½"	Border 1
	Remainder, strips 1" to 2½" wide	Freedom blocks
Pale yellow	1 square, 17½" x 17½"	Center background
Solid red	4 large-sectioned flowers	Border 2 appliqué
	3 small flowers	Border 2 appliqué
	Remainder, strips 1" to 2½" wide	Freedom blocks
Blue/print 2	2 single leaves (1 regular, 1 reversed)	Center appliqué
	4 double leaves (2 regular, 2 reversed)	Center appliqué
	Remainder, strips 1" to 2½" wide	Freedom blocks
Blue/print 3	4 squares, 2" x 2"	Border 1 corners
	Remainder, strips 1" to 2½" wide	Freedom blocks

Construct

Center Appliqué

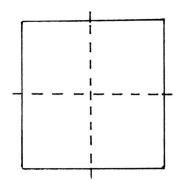

1. Lightly press the pale yellow background into quarters. This will help you to place the appliqué shapes.

2. Trace one bird and one reversed bird on the paper side of the fusible web. Rough cut around the shapes, and fuse them to the wrong side of the blue/print 1 fabric. Trim the shapes, and remove the paper. Position the shapes on the appliqué background.

3. Trace all of the single and double leaves on the paper side of the fusible web. Fuse the shapes to the blue/print 2 fabric.

4. Trace one small flower, one sectioned flower, and one reversed sectioned flower on the fusible web. Fuse the traced shapes to the red/print 2 fabric. Trim the shapes, and place the leaves and flowers on background.

5. Trace the flower center circle on fusible web, and fuse it to a small-scale dark print. Trim the shape, and place it in the center of the flower.

6. Fuse all of the shapes onto the background and appliqué in place. A blanket stitch (1.5 length x 2.0 width) and rayon decorative thread were used on the quilt shown. Make adjust-

ments to your machine as needed to accommodate different needle types, threads and stitch lengths. Secure the threads by pulling the ends to the wrong side and tying them.

7. Cut a 6" piece of red rickrack to make a circle with six points. Fold the rickrack in half and stitch a seam, keeping the edges even. Backstitch at both ends to secure the stitching. Press the seam open. Press the rickrack into a flat circle, and hide the ends of the rickrack by trimming the seam allowance and gluing ends out of sight. Make two. Use invisible thread to stitch the circles to the centers of the sectioned flowers.

8. Cut a 6" piece of blue rickrack. Press it into a curved shape to create a wing. Apply clear-drying glue to the ends of the rickrack to keep them from raveling. Make two. Place the rickrack wings on the birds; use invisible thread to stitch them in place.

Border 2 Appliqué

1. Trace four sectioned flowers on the paper side of the fusible web. Fuse the web to the wrong side of the solid red fabric. Trim the shapes, remove the paper, and center the flowers on the two 5½" yellow border corner squares. Fuse in place, and appliqué.

2. Trace four flower center circles on the paper side of the fusible web. Fuse the web to the wrong side of a small-scale dark print. Trim the shapes, remove the paper, and fuse a circle in each flower center. Appliqué the circles in place.

3. Cut 6" pieces of red rickrack. Make rickrack circles as you did for the center appliqué. Stitch the circles in place on the corner sectioned flowers.

4. For the side borders, trace 12 small flowers on the fusible web. Fuse four flowers on the wrong side of red/print 1, five flowers on the wrong side of red/print 2 and three flowers on the wrong side of the red solid.

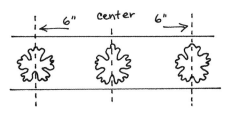

5. Trim the small flowers. Randomly mix the flowers, and fuse three on each side border. Lightly press the border in half to determine the center; place one flower on the center line. Place the other two flowers 6" from the center.

6. Appliqué the small flowers in place. If desired, cut and fuse center circles for the flowers.

Freedom Blocks
Make 24 blocks

1. Construct 24 freedom blocks that measure approximately 8" before trimming. Trim the blocks to measure 6½" x 6½". Skew 12 blocks left and 12 blocks right. Refer to Basic Techniques: Making Freedom Blocks.

Assemble

Border 1

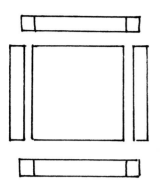

1. Stitch the side borders to the center square. Add a blue corner to each end of the top and bottom borders. Stitch the top and bottom borders to the center. Press.

Border 2

2. Stitch the side borders to the quilt top. Add a flowered corner to each end of the top and bottom borders. Stitch the top and bottom borders to the quilt top. Press.

Border 3

1. Starting with a left block in the corner, alternate laying out left- and right-skewed freedom blocks around the quilt top.

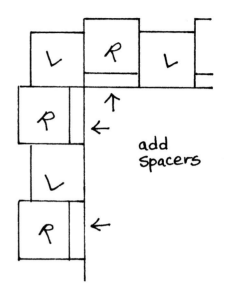

2. Stitch a yellow 1½" x 6½" spacer to the inside edge of each right freedom block as shown.

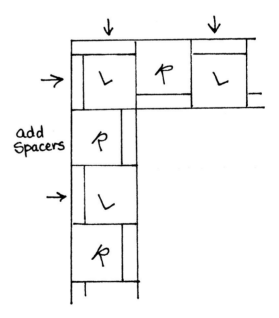

3. Stitch a medium/dark yellow 1½" x 6½" spacer to the outside edge of each left freedom block. Stitch a 1½" x 7½" spacer to the second outside edge of the four corner freedom blocks.

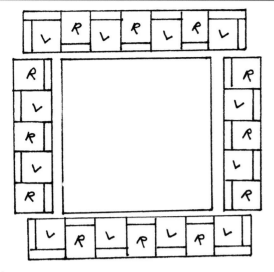

4. Stitch the side blocks together, and add them to the sides of the quilt top. Stitch the top and bottom blocks together, and add them to the top and bottom of the quilt.

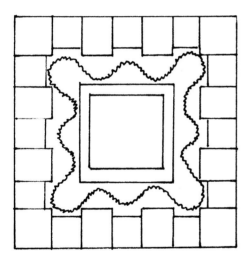

5. Cut a 146" length of rickrack. Piece the ends together to make a circle. Make sure the rickrack is twist-free before you seam the ends. Pin the rickrack loop in place, weaving in and out between the flowers. Use invisible thread to stitch the rickrack onto the quilt top.

Border 4

1. Stitch the 4" x 44½" medium/dark yellow borders to the sides of the quilt top. Stitch the 4" x 51½" medium/dark yellow borders to the top and bottom of the quilt top.

Finish

1. Piece the backing. Trim the finished backing to 54" x 54".

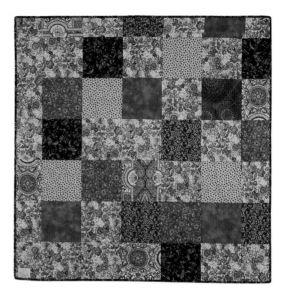

Optional Backing: For added interest, piece the backing using 8½" squares (cut size) of gaily printed fabrics. You will need 49 squares.

2. Layer the backing, batting and quilt top. Baste the layers for quilting.

3. Quilt as desired, or try these suggestions.

Center: Echo quilt each shape, and cross-hatch the background.

Border 1: Quilt ¼" from the rickrack, and stitch in the ditch between borders 1 and 2.

Border 2: Echo quilt the appliqué and rickrack.

Border 3: Try a skewed cross-hatch pattern.

Border 4: Quilt a flower vine, using the appliqué flower shapes as patterns.

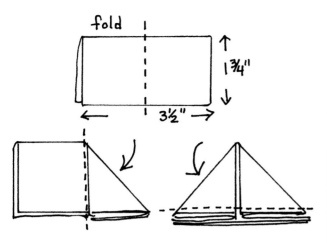

6. Add rickrack over the prairie points. Center it ¼" from the edge so that half of the rickrack will show when you stitch on your binding.

4. Add prairie points. Fold the 3½" squares of red/print 2 in half, wrong sides together. Keep the folded edge on top, and fold the right corner to the center as shown. Repeat with the left corner. All of the raw edges should now be on the bottom. Press. Baste the bottom edges of the prairie points.

5. Pin the prairie points on the right side of the quilt top, pointing to the center of the quilt. Pin 15 on each side.

7. Use the 2¼" strips for the binding; this binding was cut a little wider to accommodate the extra thickness of the prairie points and rickrack. Refer to Basic Techniques: Binding Outside Corners.

La Bohemia Notecards

Materials

Fabric

Scraps of fabrics

Other Supplies

Blank notecards and envelopes

Scraps of rickrack

Paper-backed fusible web

Appliqué pressing sheet

Pencil

Small, sharp scissors

La Bohemia Notecard
Templates on Page 126

Send a bit of cheer and old-world romance when you write a message on your La Bohemia Notecards. Mix and match the flowers and birds to make these creative notes with bits of fabric left from your La Bohemia Wall Quilt. Relax, cut the shapes, and fuse the fabrics to blank notecards. If the fabrics inspire you, fussy cut designs directly from the fabric, and have fun arranging original motifs.

Construct and Assemble

1. Make a practice card first to test the compatibility of your materials. Follow the manufacturer's directions for your fusible web. I liked the option of using Lite Steam-A-Seam2 to temporarily stick the shapes in place before fusing them.

2. Trace the shapes onto the paper side of the fusible web. Fuse the shapes to the wrong side of the selected fabrics. Trim the shapes, and position them on the notecards.

Finish

1. Cover the card with an appliqué pressing sheet. Fuse the fabric shapes in place.

2. If the cards curl when heated by your iron, place them under books or magazines — quilting magazines, of course — to flatten them.

Patterns

4" Star Paper-Piecing Foundations

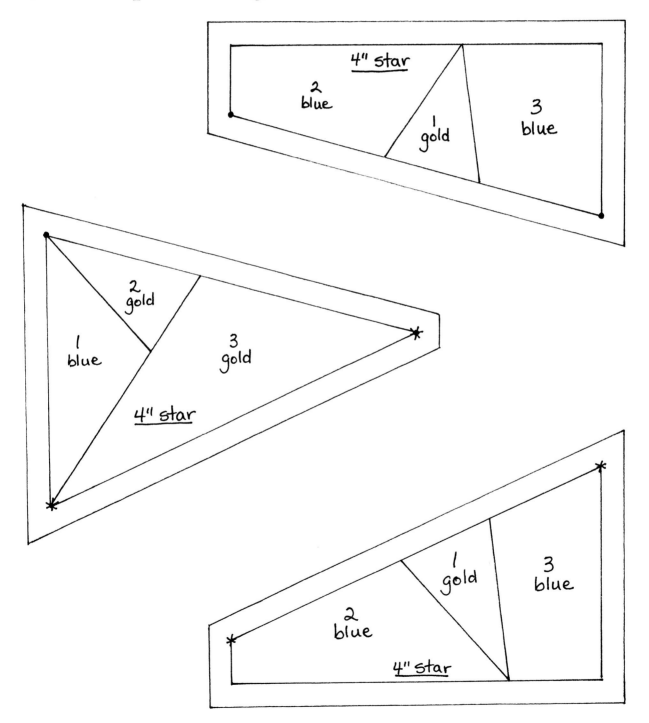

5" Star Paper-Piecing Foundations

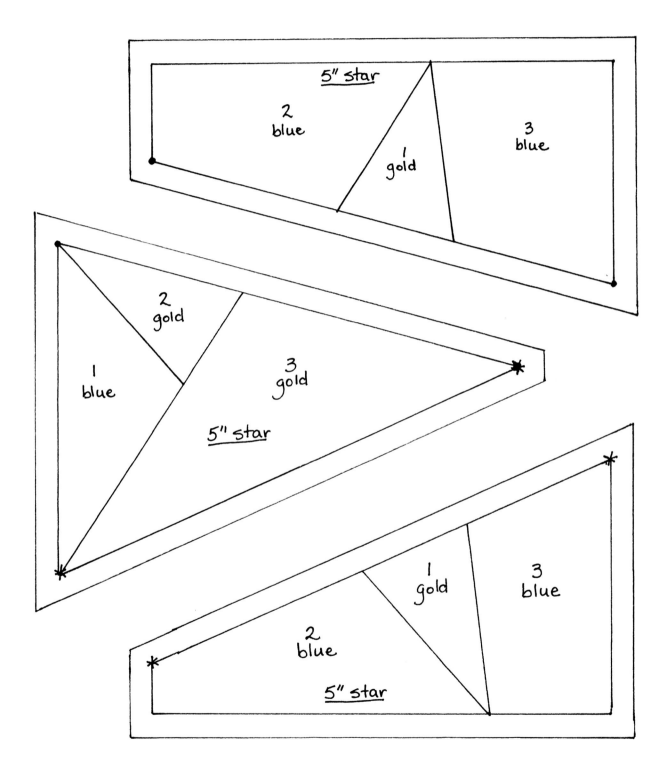

Day Away Mat Templates

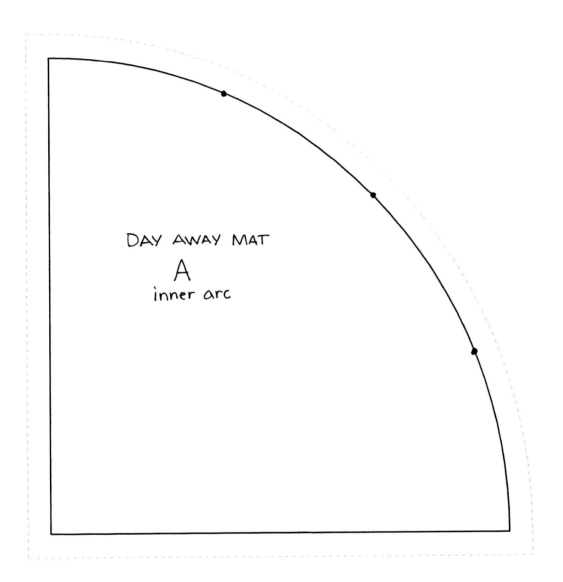

DAY AWAY MAT

A

inner arc

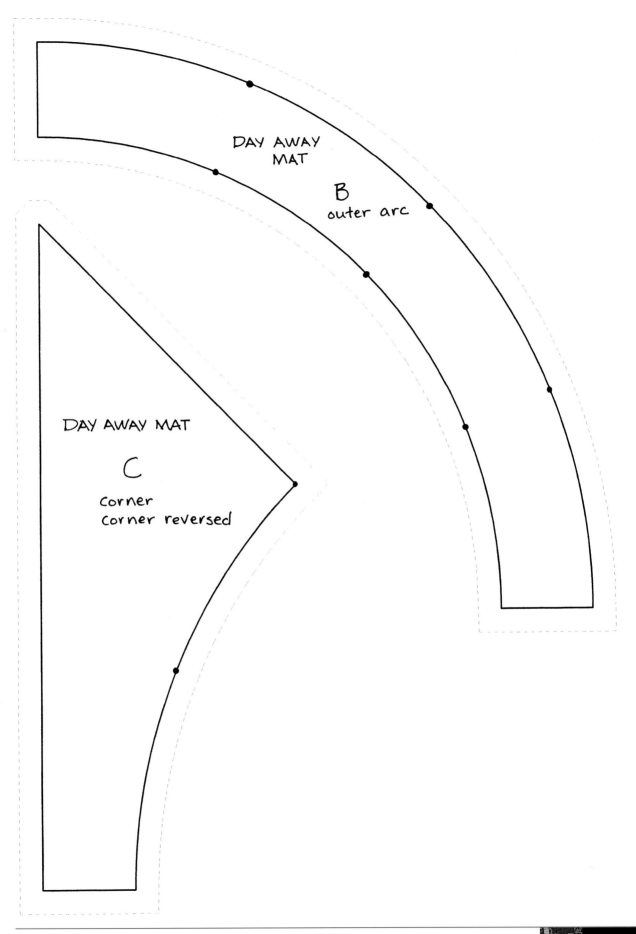

DAY AWAY
MAT

B
outer arc

DAY AWAY MAT

C

corner
corner reversed

Let the Seeds Fall Where They May Templates

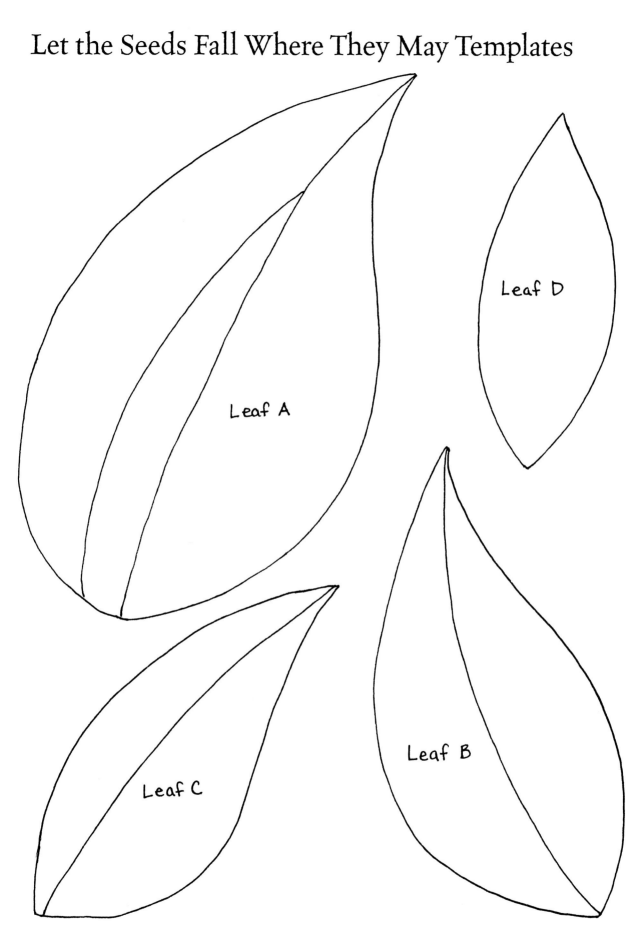

Leaf A

Leaf D

Leaf C

Leaf B

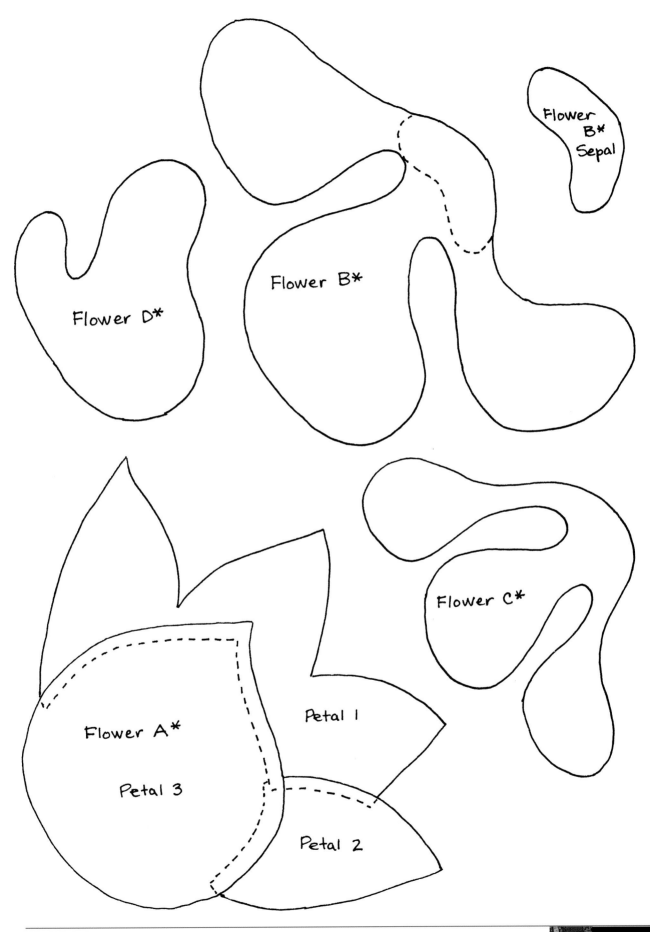

Flower B* Sepal

Flower D*

Flower B*

Flower C*

Flower A*

Petal 3

Petal 1

Petal 2

La Bohemia Quilt Templates

La Bohemia Notecard Templates

Contributors

Tools & Notions

Clover Needlecraft Inc.
Sewing and quilting notions,
cutting tools and specialty products.
13438 Alondra Blvd. • Cerritos, CA 90703
E-mail: cni@clover-usa.com
Web: www.clover-usa.com

June Tailor
Cutting tools, sewing and quilting notions and
related products.
P.O. Box 208 • Richfield, WI 53076
Phone: (800) 844-5400
E-mail: customerservice@junetailor.com
Web: www.junetailor.com

Prym Consumer USA
Sewing, quilting, cutting and craft-related tools
and notions.
P.O. Box 5028 • Spartanburg, SC 29304
Web: www.dritz.com

Sulky of America Inc.
Threads, stabilizers and spray adhesives.
P.O. Box 494129 • Port Charlotte, FL 33949-4129
Phone: (800) 874-4115
E-mail: info@sulky.com
Web: www.sulky.com

Wrights
EZ Quilting tools, trims and embellishments.
85 South St. • P.O. Box 398
West Warren, MA 01092
Phone: (800) 660-0415
Web: www.wrights.com

Fabric & Batting

Hobbs Bonded Fibers
Battings, pillow inserts
and fiberfill.
P.O. Box 2521 • Waco, TX 76702-2521
Phone: (800) 433-3357
Web: www.hobbsbondedfibers.com

Michael Miller Fabrics LLC
Fabrics for quilting, sewing and crafts.
118 W. 22nd St., 5th Floor • New York, NY 10011
Phone: (212) 704-0774
Fax: (212) 633-0272
E-mail: info@michaelmillerfabrics.com
Web: www.michaelmillerfabrics.com

Robert Kaufman Co. Inc.
Fabric supplier and converter of quilting fabrics
and textiles for manufacturers.
129 W. 132nd St. • Los Angeles, CA 90061
Phone: (800) 877-2066
E-mail: info@robertkaufman.com
Web: www.robertkaufman.com

The Warm Co.
Batting and fusible products.
954 E. Union St. • Seattle, WA 98122
Phone: (800) 234-9276
E-mail: info@warmcompany.com
Web: www.warmcompany.com

Contributors

Photography Locations

Golden Eagle Log Homes

Manufacturer of quality log homes.
4421 Plover Road • Wisconsin Rapids, WI 54494
Phone: (800) 270-5025
E-mail: goldnegl@wctc.net
Web: www.goldeneagleloghomes.com

Furniture and Appliancemart Superstore

Name-brand furniture, appliances, electronics and bedding.
3349 Church St. • Stevens Point, WI 54481
Phone: (715) 344-7700
Web: www.furnitureappliancemart.com

Publishing

Krause Publications

Publisher of this and other quality how-to books for sewing, quilting, machine embroidery and other crafts.
700 E. State St. • Iola, WI 54990-0001
Phone: (888) 457-2873
Web: www.krause.com

Quilt Hangers

Lorie's Little Quilts

Manufacturer of a variety of oak quilt hangers.
241 County Road 120 • Carthage, MO 64836
Phone: (888) 419-5618
E-mail: lorie@lorieslittlequilts.com
Web: www.lorieslittlequilts.com

Useful Resources

Annie's Attic
Web: www.anniesattic.com

Clotilde LLC
Web: www.clotilde.com

Connecting Threads
Web: www.ConnectingThreads.com

Ghee's
Web: www.ghees.com

Herrschners Inc.
Web: www.herrschners.com

Home Sew
Web: www.homesew.com

Keepsake Quilting
Web: www.keepsakequilting.com

Nancy's Notions
Web: www.nancysnotions.com